Cake Icing and Decorating

Cake
Icing and
Decorating
Pamela Dotter

Sundial

Contents

First published in 1978 by Sundial publications Limited
59 Grosvenor Street, London W1

Twelfth Impression, 1981

© 1978 Hennerwood Publications Limited

ISBN 0 904230 64 3

Printed in Hong Kong

Introduction

After the serious business of feeding the family, you can enjoy yourself creating a fancy cake. Not that it's a frivolous occupation; a beautifully decorated cake plays an important part in many celebrations, starting with Christenings and carrying on through to Golden Weddings. But all celebrations are not formal and there is also the opportunity to create a fun cake for a child's birthday party.

You will find ideas for cakes for every occasion in this book. Some require much time and skill, but there are many others that can be fitted into the busiest programme.

Cake icing and decorating appeals to the artist in us all. With dull automated jobs in both the factory and the home, many people look for a craft for their leisure time. Cake icing and decorating is just such an activity. After all, cakes can be eaten without being adorned with icing; but how much nicer they are when they appeal to the senses as well as the palate.

The recipes and clear step-by-step instructions in this book will help you to develop your skills, and there are many designs illustrated to inspire you. Start with a gâteau and work up to a wedding cake. Have confidence in your abilities. This is the best way to acquire a steady hand for piping.

In studying the designs of cakes on the following pages you will see that most of them are regular geometric shapes. This is because a cake must look good from every angle. Once you have mastered the basic steps, create your own designs. Look in confectioners' windows for inspiration for gâteaux and royal iced cakes.

Children's story books will give ideas for novelty cakes. Keep designs simple and colours delicate to show off the perfection of the icing. Don't get too carried away and forget that the cake must look edible. Take every opportunity to produce a decorated cake, because practice is an essential ingredient to success. Check your standard by entering a local show. There's nothing like a bit of competition to bring out the best in most people.

When you are spending time making a cake look beautiful remember that it will be eaten, so make sure the base is worthy of that decoration. In the cake recipe chapter you will find recipes for good quality cakes for every occasion, with instructions for baking them in various shapes and sizes.

Cake icing and decorating is a rewarding skill that can be developed into an absorbing hobby. Many happy and rewarding hours can be spent following the designs in this book. Enjoy yourself.

Note: do make sure all your equipment is scrupulously clean, sterilising such items as hat pins before use (by holding in a match flame or boiling water). This is especially important when decorating cakes that are stored for some time, and for very perishable gâteaux.

DECORATING EQUIPMENT

The right equipment makes a job so much easier, especially with a skilled job where a high standard of finish is required. But there's no need to spend a fortune, though it is worthwhile buying good quality equipment.

General kitchen equipment: You will need an earthenware or glass bowl, not metal which would discolour the icing. It must have a good surface, because minute cracks could harbour grease which would harm Royal icing. Small bowls with airtight seals are useful for storing Royal icing and separating coloured icings. Treat yourself to a new wooden spoon for beating Royal icing and keep it exclusively for that job. Any wooden spoon will do for Butter icing, but make sure it hasn't been used for stirring highly-flavoured foods like onions. Scissors, string, a spatula, a sieve and a pastry brush will probably already be in the kitchen. You will also need a palette knife and some measuring spoons — metric spoons graduated from 2.5 ml to 15 ml are well worth having. A pair of compasses from a geometry set is useful for marking designs as are artists' fine paint brushes.

Cake tins: Good quality tins last for years. They keep their shape and make well-shaped cakes. Buy tins that are of regular 2.5 cm (1 inch) measurements so that you can achieve an accurate 5 cm (2 inch) difference in size between tiers of wedding cakes and cake boards. Make sure the sides are not sloping. Always measure tins from the base. Tins are available in various shapes: heart, horseshoe, hexagonal and in numerals. These can all be obtained from specialist cake icing centres.

Cake boards: Attractive silver boards are available from stationers, though very large sizes or gold-covered boards may only be available from specialist centres. Use 1.25 cm (½ inch) thick boards for large cakes and the thinner cake cards for gâteaux. Oblong cake cards are available for Swiss rolls and bar cakes.

Turntable: You can manage without one of these, unless you intend to do a lot of Royal iced cakes. Choose a heavy turntable that is stable when tilted. For the occasional iced cake, use an upturned plate instead.

Straight edge icing ruler: This is a heavy, unmarked length of stainless steel for smoothing the top of a Royal iced cake. Its smooth edge and heavy quality ensure that the icing is really smooth. A new ruler would be the best substitute, but the graduations will be noticeable on the finished surface.

Plastic scrapers: Use for smoothing the sides of Royal iced cakes or for quickly obtaining a smooth surface on a Butter iced cake. They are available with a smooth or a serrated edge. Use the rounded side of the scraper for cleaning out bowls.

Waxed, greaseproof and non-stick papers: Buy the best quality possible; use for piping bags and icing run-out decorations (see pages 36–37).

Cake decorations and special ingredients: Silver leaves, horseshoes, cake pillars, special figures, novelty candle holders and emblems for cakes are available at specialist shops and cake icing centres. Concentrated cake colourings, egg albumen, glucose liquid, mallow icing for moulding and special almond paste are available from major cake icing centres by mail order (see inside back cover).

Piping equipment

Piping tubes

Piping tubes can be bought at good hardware stores, shops selling catering equipment and cake icing centres (see inside back cover). They are available in both plastic and metal.

Plastic tubes are very useful for large Savoy tubes for piping cream, meringues and éclairs, also for the large star and writing tubes for Butter icing. They cannot become damaged during storage and are very easy to keep clean. For fine work, and the sharpest definition, metal tubes are best.

Piping tubes can have screw ends for attaching to an icing syringe or be smooth for fitting into a piping bag. An icing syringe is useful for Butter icing, but it is difficult to control and achieve a fine design; it is also quite tiring to use. Smooth ended tubes used with piping bags are the most satisfactory.

Savoy tubes: These large tubes are available in both plain and star designs numbered from 3 to 15. Use them for whipped cream, Butter icing, meringues, éclairs, macaroons, biscuits and creamed potato for savoury dishes. Washable fabric or nylon bags are used with these tubes, available in sizes from 30 cm (12 inch) to 50 cm (20 inch).

Writing tubes: Small plain tubes are available from very fine (size 0) to thick (size 4). A number 2 and a number 4 would comprise a basic set. Use for lines, lattices, beads and scribbling.

Star tubes: There are many sizes available. A basic set would be a number 6 and a number 8. Use for stars, shells, whirls and scrolls.

Scroll tubes: These have finer points than star tubes. Use for stars, scrolls, shells and whirls.

Ribbon tube: Use this flat serrated tube for a basket design or an edging.

Petal tubes: These are curved with a fine and a thicker side. Use for making sugar roses and leaves.

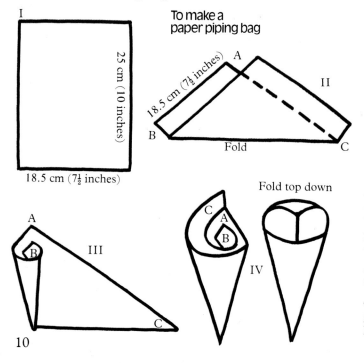

To make a
paper piping bag

I

25 cm (10 inches)

18.5 cm (7½ inches)

18.5 cm (7½ inches)

A

B

C

Fold

II

A

B

III

C

C

A

B

IV

Fold top down

Piping bags

For Butter icing, where a large quantity of icing may be used, use a large piping bag with a screw adaptor which converts the bag for use with a small tube. The tube can be easily replaced for another with this adaptor.

For fine work, and always when piping with Royal icing, use a paper piping bag. Good quality greaseproof paper or non-stick silicone paper should be used. Piping bags can be bought ready made but they are very quick to make once you have the knack. Use a very small bag for fine work for the most control. Large bags split easily.

To make a paper piping bag: Take a standard sized oblong sheet of greaseproof paper and cut it into four to make oblongs of 25 cm × 18.5 cm (10 inches × 7½ inches) as in diagram I. Fold as shown in diagram II. Cut along the fold. With the longest side of one triangle at the bottom, form a cone shape by curving B underneath point A at the top (diagram III). Hold firmly and wrap the paper round until point C is behind point A (diagram IV). Fold all the points together. The point of the cone should be very sharp. If there is a hole at the bottom, push the inner point upwards.

For Butter icing, cut each sheet of greaseproof paper into two oblongs, and make only four piping bags.

To fit a piping tube: Snip off the end of the cone and drop in the tube. It should protrude about ⅓ of its length.

To fill a piping bag: Hold the bag at the top with the thumb half way down the bag. Place the icing in the bag with a small palette knife and clean it off against the bag where it is held. Close the top, then fold in each side and fold the top down. Hold the bag between the first two fingers and press out the icing with the thumb.

Using piping tubes

A whole range of designs can be piped using a selection of tubes and greaseproof paper or nylon piping bags.

As with most craft skills, practice is required before the beginner attempts a cake. Start off with mashed potato using a large star tube and a nylon piping bag, then progress to Butter icing using a greaseproof paper bag. Next try Royal icing, starting with the thick, plain tubes and progressing to the finer ones. Always practise the design on an upturned plate before starting on a cake, to make sure that the icing is of the correct consistency.

Piping with Butter icing: Add hot water, a drop at a time, to make the icing fairly soft. It must be softer for use in a plain tube than a star tube. You cannot pipe Butter icing with a fine writing tube; a number 4 must be used.

Piping with cream: Use whipping cream or a mixture of double and single creams for piping. The consistency must be very soft; the cream should just hold its shape after whipping. Piping makes the cream go buttery and the design 'frilly'. Use a large star or plain tube and nylon piping bag. Put only a few spoonfuls of softly whipped cream into the bag and pipe part of the design. As soon as it starts to go 'frilly' round the edges, wash out the bag and start again.

Top row: Fine scroll tubes, Nos. 44, 43, 42; No. 1 writing
Middle row: No. 58 petal; No. 22 ribbon; No. 8 star; No. 6 small star
Bottom row: Savoy star tubes: large, medium, small

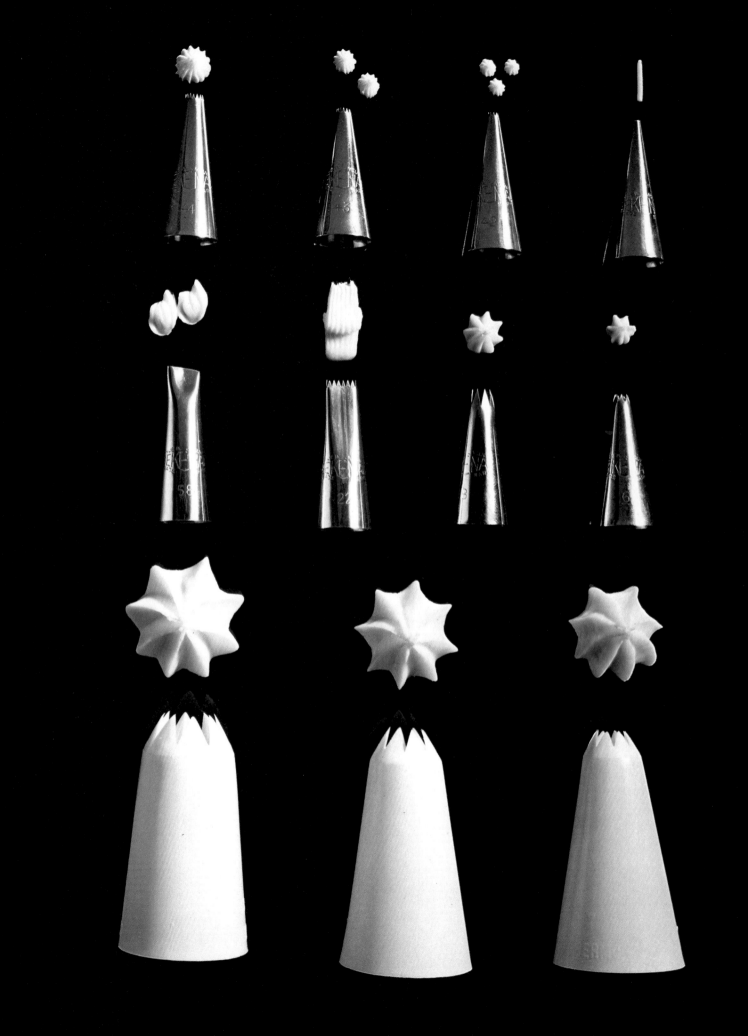

Lemon snow cake: made from two 18 cm (7 inch) whisked sponge cakes. Sandwich and cover with lemon-flavoured Butter icing, made from 225 g (8 oz) icing sugar. Make the top design by working grooves in the icing with a small palette knife; pull the icing into peaks for the side decoration. Decorate the top edge with orange and lemon slices cut into triangles

Daisy chain cake: made from a Vanilla torten sponge cake baked in a round 20 cm (8 inch) tin. Layer with apricot jam and coat the top and side in Rich butter cream. Make the ridged design with a serrated scraper and decorate the top in a flower design in the centre and a chain design round the edge with sections of glacé cherries and diamond-shaped pieces of candied angelica. Use mimosa balls to form the flower centres

Mocha marshmallow bar: made from an 18 cm (7 inch) square Quick mix cake cut in half. Layer and cover with Marshmallow butter icing flavoured with 1 × 5 ml spoon (1 teaspoon) instant coffee powder and 50 g (2 oz) melted plain chocolate. Make the lattice design on the top by pressing a skewer into instant coffee or cocoa powder and pressing on the surface of the icing. Decorate the edge with halved chocolate buttons

Iced cup cakes: made from a 100 g (4 oz) quantity of Quick mix cake batter baked in 18 paper cases. Decorate with Glacé icing and assorted sweets, candied angelica cut into diamonds and glacé cherries.
  To make the feather iced design, put a little deep pink Glacé icing into a paper piping bag without a tube. Ice the cakes, then quickly snip off the point of the bag and pipe a thread of icing on each cake in a spiral or a line. Draw a skewer through the icing from the centre to the edge or from side to side, reversing the direction each time

ICINGS, FILLINGS AND FROSTINGS

Icings can be smooth or fudgy, rich or fluffy — whatever will complement the cake and is to your taste. Some can be coloured and moulded to make cake decorations.

Butter icing

Metric	Imperial
100 g butter or margarine	4 oz butter or margarine
200 g icing sugar, sifted	8 oz icing sugar, sifted
2 × 5 ml spoons lemon juice	2 teaspoons lemon juice

Place the butter or margarine in a bowl and beat with a wooden spoon until light and fluffy. Add the icing sugar and lemon juice and beat until smooth. Flavour as for Rich butter cream.

Marshmallow butter icing

Metric	Imperial
2 egg whites	2 egg whites
100 g icing sugar, sifted	4 oz icing sugar, sifted
125 g unsalted butter, softened	5 oz unsalted butter, softened

Put the egg whites in a clean grease-free heatproof bowl. Add the icing sugar and place the bowl over a saucepan of hot but not boiling water. Whisk until the mixture thickens and leaves a trail when the whisk is lifted. Remove the bowl from the saucepan and continue to whisk until the meringue mixture stands up in peaks and is cool.
Place the butter in a bowl and beat until it is light and fluffy. Add the meringue a little at a time, whisking well after each addition. Add flavourings if required.
To Flavour:
Chocolate: Add 50 g (2 oz) melted plain chocolate.
Coffee: Add 1 × 15 ml spoon (1 tablespoon) coffee essence or 1 × 5 ml spoon (1 teaspoon) instant coffee powder dissolved in 1 × 15 ml spoon (1 tablespoon) boiling water.
Orange or Lemon: Add 1 × 5 ml spoon (1 teaspoon) grated orange or lemon rind and 1 × 15 ml spoon (1 tablespoon) juice. Add yellow or orange colourings.

Rich butter cream

Metric	Imperial
50 g sugar	2 oz sugar
125 ml water	¼ pint water
1 egg yolk	1 egg yolk
150 g unsalted butter	5 oz unsalted butter

Put the sugar and water in a saucepan and heat gently, stirring to dissolve the sugar. Bring to the boil and boil for 3 minutes, without stirring.
Place a little of the syrup on the backs of 2 teaspoons. Press the spoons together and pull apart; if a thread forms between the spoons the syrup is ready. If not, return to the heat and boil for a further 1 to 2 minutes and retest.
Place the egg yolk in a bowl and gradually whisk in the syrup. Continue to whisk until the mixture is cool.
Cut the butter into small pieces and whisk into the egg mixture a little at a time, whisking well after each addition. Add flavouring, if required.
To Flavour:
Chocolate: Add 1 × 5 ml spoon (1 teaspoon) cocoa powder to the water, then whisk 25 g (1 oz) chopped plain chocolate into the egg with the syrup.
Coffee: Add 1 × 5 ml spoon (1 teaspoon) instant coffee powder to the water.
Lemon or Orange: Add the grated rind of 1 lemon or orange, 4 × 15 ml spoons (4 tablespoons) juice, and yellow or orange food colouring to the finished icing.
Praline: Add finely crushed praline made by boiling 50 g (2 oz) sugar with 2 × 15 ml spoons (2 tablespoons) water until golden brown. Add 50 g (2 oz) shelled (but not skinned) almonds or hazelnuts, then quickly pour onto an oiled baking sheet. When cold, crush with a rolling pin or pulverise in an electric grinder and add to the finished icing.
Vanilla: Add 1 × 2.5 ml spoon (½ teaspoon) vanilla essence to the basic mixture.

Glacé icing

Metric	Imperial
250 g icing sugar, sifted	10 oz icing sugar, sifted
3 × 15 ml spoons boiling water	3 tablespoons boiling water
Food colouring	Food colouring

Put the icing sugar in a bowl and gradually stir in the water until the icing thickly coats the back of the spoon. Add a few drops of food colouring if desired.
To Flavour:
Orange or Lemon: Replace the boiling water with orange or lemon juice.
Coffee: Dissolve 1 × 5 ml spoon (1 teaspoon) instant coffee powder in the boiling water.
Chocolate: Melt 75 g (3 oz) chopped plain chocolate in a saucepan with the water, remove from the heat and beat in the icing sugar, 1 × 2.5 ml spoon (½ teaspoon) oil and 2 drops of vanilla essence.

Rose petal ring cake: made in a ring tin with a 100 g (4 oz) quantity of Quick mix cake mixture. Cover the cake with Quick American frosting and decorate the top with frosted rose petals and leaves

Chocolate swirl cake: made from a 3-egg quantity of chocolate-flavoured Whisked sponge cake baked in a 20 cm (8 inch) round cake tin. Layer the cake with vanilla-flavoured Butter icing and cover with Chocolate fudge frosting.
Swirl the icing and arrange three groups of 5 blanched almond halves in a flower design. Place a piece of crystallized rose in the centre of each

Butter fudge cake: made from a 100 g (4 oz) quantity of Quick mix cake batter baked in an 18 cm (7 inch) square tin. Fill the cake with chocolate-flavoured Butter icing and cover with Fudge frosting. Decorate with chocolate curls

Chocolate fudge frosting

Metric

100 g plain chocolate
50 g butter
1 egg, beaten
175 g icing sugar, sifted

Imperial

4 oz plain chocolate
2 oz butter
1 egg, beaten
6 oz icing sugar, sifted

Break up the chocolate and put in a heatproof bowl with the butter. Place the bowl over a saucepan of hot but not boiling water and melt the chocolate, stirring occasionally. Stir in the egg, then remove from the saucepan. Add the icing sugar and beat with a wooden spoon until the frosting is smooth.
Use the frosting to fill and cover cakes, swirling the top and sides with a palette knife. Leave to set for several hours, then decorate as desired.
For a smooth coating icing, use only 100 g (4 oz) icing sugar and pour over the cake.
Sufficient to fill and frost a 20 cm ((8 inch) cake

Quick American frosting

Metric

175 g caster sugar
1 egg white
2 × 15 ml spoons hot water
Pinch of cream of tartar
Food colouring (optional)

Imperial

6 oz caster sugar
1 egg white
2 tablespoons hot water
Pinch of cream of tartar
Food colouring (optional)

Put all the ingredients, except the food colouring, in a heatproof bowl and place over a saucepan of hot but not boiling water. Whisk until the mixture thickens and soft peaks form when the whisk is lifted.
Remove the bowl from the saucepan, add a few drops of food colouring, if desired, and whisk until the mixture is evenly coloured.
Use the frosting to fill and cover cakes. Spread quickly over the cake and form into swirls or peaks with a small palette knife. Leave to set.
Sufficient to fill and frost a 20 cm (8 inch) cake

Fudge frosting

Metric

75 g butter
3 × 15 ml spoons milk
25 g soft brown sugar
1 × 15 ml spoon black treacle
300 g icing sugar, sifted

Imperial

3 oz butter
3 tablespoons milk
1 oz soft brown sugar
1 tablespoon black treacle
12 oz icing sugar, sifted

Put the butter, milk, brown sugar and treacle in a heatproof bowl over a saucepan of hot but not boiling water. Stir occasionally until the butter and sugar have melted, then remove the bowl from the saucepan. Stir in the icing sugar, then beat with a wooden spoon until the icing is smooth.
Pour quickly over a cake for a smooth coating, or leave to cool and then spread over a cake and swirl with a small palette knife. Leave frosting to set, then decorate as desired.
Sufficient to fill and frost a 20 cm (8 inch) cake

Variations:
For a creamy-coloured frosting replace brown sugar with caster sugar and black treacle with golden syrup. Flavour with the grated rind of 1 lemon or orange or 2 × 5 ml spoons (2 teaspoons) instant coffee powder.

Above: *Woodland cake:* cover an 18 cm (7 inch) Rich fruit cake with Almond paste and then Gelatine icing. Colour the trimmings and mould to make toadstools, rabbits and chicks (see pages 24–25). Fit a cake frill around the side

Circles celebration cake: cover a 20 cm (8 inch) Rich fruit cake with Almond paste and then Moulding icing. Colour the trimmings green and yellow; cut out some circles with a small round cutter and cut others into squares. Arrange them alternately in two circles on top of the cake, securing with a little Glacé icing. Fit a matching ribbon around the side

Orange satin bar: made from an 18 cm (7 inch) square cake, cut in half and layered with marmalade. Cover with orange-flavoured and coloured Satin icing. Colour the trimmings a deeper orange and form into a plait for the top and a rope for the bottom edge

1. Roll out Moulding Icing to a circle 5 cm (2 inches) larger than the cake

2. Support the icing on a rolling pin and place over the top of the cake

3. Press the icing onto the side of the cake, working surplus icing to the base of the board. Dip your hands in cornflour and rub the surface in a circular movement. Cut off the excess icing

1

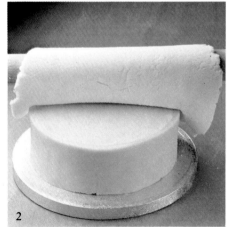

2

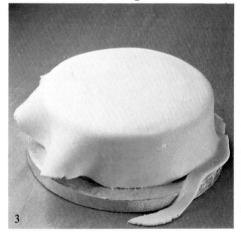

3

Moulding icing

Metric	Imperial
450 g icing sugar, sifted	1 lb icing sugar, sifted
1 egg white	1 egg white
1 rounded 15 ml spoon glucose liquid or syrup	1 rounded tablespoon glucose liquid or syrup

Put the icing sugar in a bowl. Add the egg white and glucose and mix together with a wooden spoon, then knead well with your fingers until the mixture forms a ball.

Sprinkle a work surface with cornflour. Knead the icing on the surface until smooth and pliable. If the icing is too firm add a few drops of water and knead well.

Keep the icing in a well-sealed polythene bag to prevent drying. If the icing becomes dry on the surface, dip quickly into hot water, replace in the bag, leave 1 hour, then knead again.

Use this icing, coloured as required, to mould decorations or to cover the top and side of a cake (see pictures).

Sufficient to cover a 20 cm (8 inch) round cake

Satin icing

Metric	Imperial
25 g butter or margarine	1 oz butter or margarine
1 × 15 ml spoon lemon juice	1 tablespoon lemon juice
1 × 15 ml spoon water	1 tablespoon water
About 300 g icing sugar, sifted	About 12 oz icing sugar, sifted
Food colouring (optional)	Food colouring (optional)

Put the butter or margarine, lemon juice and water in a saucepan and heat gently until the fat has melted. Add 100 g (4 oz) of the icing sugar and stir over a low heat until dissolved. Cook for 2 minutes or until the mixture begins to boil gently (do not overcook or the icing will be too hard).

Remove from the heat and add another 100 g (4 oz) of the icing sugar. Beat with a wooden spoon until well mixed, then turn the mixture into a bowl. Gradually beat in enough of the remaining icing sugar to make the icing the consistency of a soft dough.

Turn out onto a work surface lightly dusted with icing sugar and knead until smooth. Colour with food colouring if desired.

Keep in a well-sealed polythene bag to avoid drying out. If the icing does dry on the surface, dip quickly into hot water, replace in the bag, leave for 1 hour, then knead again.

Use this icing to mould decorations or to cover the top and side of a cake.

Sufficient to cover a 17 cm (7 inch) round cake

Note: If icing is required very white, use white fat instead of butter or margarine.

Gelatine icing

Metric	Imperial
2 × 5 ml spoons powdered gelatine	2 teaspoons powdered gelatine
2 × 15 ml spoons water	2 tablespoons water
450 g icing sugar, sifted	1 lb icing sugar, sifted
1 egg white	1 egg white
2 × 5 ml spoons glycerine	2 teaspoons glycerine
Food colouring (optional)	Food colouring (optional)

Put the gelatine and water in a heatproof bowl. Place over a saucepan of hot but not boiling water and dissolve the gelatine, stirring occasionally. Remove from the saucepan and allow to cool.

Put the icing sugar in another bowl and add the dissolved gelatine, egg white and glycerine. Mix together with a wooden spoon to form a dough. Knead until smooth, adding more icing sugar if necessary. Colour as desired.

Keep in a well-sealed polythene bag to avoid drying out. If the icing becomes dry on the surface, dip quickly into hot water, replace in the bag, leave for 1 hour, then knead again.

Use this icing to make cut-out decorations or to cover the top and side of a cake.

Sufficient to cover a 20 cm (8 inch) round cake

CAKE RECIPES

Here are recipes for most of the cakes that you will need as bases for the iced cakes in the book. There are full instructions for baking them in various shapes and sizes and adding flavourings.

Rich fruit cake

Metric

Size of cake in cm	Round 15 Square 12.5	Round 17.5 Square 15	Round 20 Square 17.5	Round 22.5 Square 20	Round 25 Square 22.5	Round 27.5 Square 25	Round 30 Square 27.5	Round 32.5 Square 30
Currants	150 g	200 g	275 g	375 g	500 g	550 g	700 g	800 g
Sultanas	75 g	100 g	175 g	200 g	250 g	350 g	375 g	400 g
Raisins	40 g	50 g	75 g	100 g	125 g	150 g	175 g	225 g
Glacé cherries, halved	40 g	50 g	75 g	100 g	125 g	150 g	175 g	225 g
Mixed cut peel	40 g	50 g	75 g	100 g	125 g	150 g	175 g	225 g
Mixed chopped nuts	40 g	50 g	75 g	100 g	125 g	150 g	175 g	200 g
Grated lemon rind (5 ml spoons)	$\frac{3}{4}$	1	$1\frac{1}{2}$	2	$2\frac{1}{2}$	3	$3\frac{1}{2}$	4
Brandy (15 ml spoons) (optional)	1	$1\frac{1}{2}$	2	$2\frac{1}{2}$	$3\frac{1}{2}$	4	5	6
Plain flour	90 g	125 g	200 g	250 g	300 g	400 g	450 g	500 g
Mixed spice (5 ml spoons)	$\frac{3}{4}$	1	$1\frac{1}{2}$	$1\frac{3}{4}$	2	3	$3\frac{1}{2}$	4
Ground almonds	25 g	25 g	50 g	50 g	75 g	75 g	100 g	100 g
Soft brown sugar	75 g	100 g	175 g	225 g	275 g	325 g	400 g	450 g
Butter, softened	75 g	100 g	175 g	225 g	275 g	325 g	400 g	450 g
Black treacle (15 ml spoons)	$\frac{1}{2}$	1	1	$1\frac{1}{2}$	2	2	3	4
Eggs	2	3	4	5	7	8	10	12

Imperial

Size of cake in inches	Round 6 Square 5	Round 7 Square 6	Round 8 Square 7	Round 9 Square 8	Round 10 Square 9	Round 11 Square 10	Round 12 Square 11	Round 13 Square 12
Currants	5 oz	7 oz	10 oz	13 oz	1 lb	1 lb 2 oz	1 lb 7 oz	$1\frac{3}{4}$ lb
Sultanas	3 oz	4 oz	6 oz	7 oz	9 oz	12 oz	14 oz	1 lb
Raisins	$1\frac{1}{2}$ oz	2 oz	3 oz	$3\frac{1}{2}$ oz	$4\frac{1}{2}$ oz	6 oz	7 oz	8 oz
Glacé cherries, halved	$1\frac{1}{2}$ oz	2 oz	3 oz	$3\frac{1}{2}$ oz	$4\frac{1}{2}$ oz	6 oz	7 oz	8 oz
Mixed cut peel	$1\frac{1}{2}$ oz	2 oz	3 oz	$3\frac{1}{2}$ oz	$4\frac{1}{2}$ oz	6 oz	7 oz	8 oz
Mixed chopped nuts	$1\frac{1}{2}$ oz	2 oz	3 oz	$3\frac{1}{2}$ oz	$4\frac{1}{2}$ oz	6 oz	7 oz	8 oz
Grated lemon rind (teaspoons)	$\frac{3}{4}$	1	$1\frac{1}{2}$	2	$2\frac{1}{2}$	3	$3\frac{1}{2}$	4
Brandy (tablespoons) (optional)	1	$1\frac{1}{2}$	2	$2\frac{1}{2}$	$3\frac{1}{2}$	4	5	6
Plain flour	$3\frac{1}{2}$ oz	5 oz	7 oz	9 oz	11 oz	14 oz	1 lb	1 lb 4 oz
Mixed spice (teaspoons)	$\frac{3}{4}$	1	$1\frac{1}{2}$	$1\frac{3}{4}$	2	3	$3\frac{1}{2}$	4
Ground almonds	1 oz	1 oz	2 oz	2 oz	$2\frac{1}{2}$ oz	3 oz	$3\frac{1}{2}$ oz	4 oz
Soft brown sugar	3 oz	4 oz	6 oz	8 oz	9 oz	12 oz	14 oz	1 lb
Butter, softened	3 oz	4 oz	6 oz	8 oz	9 oz	12 oz	14 oz	1 lb
Black treacle (tablespoons)	$\frac{1}{2}$	1	1	$1\frac{1}{2}$	2	2	3	4
Eggs	2	3	4	5	7	8	10	12

Cooking time: see method
Oven: 140°C, 275°F, Gas Mark 1

Wrap a piece of greaseproof paper around the tin and cut off the overlap. The paper should extend 7.5 cm (3 inches) above the rim of the tin, so cut off any excess. Cut another piece of paper the same size. Cut two circles the size of the base of the tin. Grease the tin thoroughly with melted lard. Fold over 2.5 cm (1 inch) of the long paper strip and make cuts along the fold, about 2.5 cm (1 inch) apart. Place in the tin with the fold on the base. Press the paper to the side of the tin to prevent bubbles. Brush the paper with melted lard and press one circle in the base. Press down well. Repeat with the other pieces of paper. Tie a double thick strip of brown paper around the outside of the tin.

Line a square cake tin in a similar way. Snip the fold at the corners only.

Put the currants, sultanas and raisins in a large mixing bowl. Halve the cherries and add to the bowl with the mixed peel, chopped nuts, finely grated lemon rind and brandy (if used). Mix together until all the fruit is well mixed and coated in brandy. (Cover and leave overnight, if desired.) Sift the flour and mixed spice into another mixing bowl. Add the ground almonds, sugar and butter. Measure the treacle carefully, levelling the spoon with a knife and making sure there is none on the underside of the spoon. Add to the bowl with the eggs. Mix together with a wooden spoon and beat for 2 to 3 minutes by hand, or 1 to 2 minutes with a mixer, until the mixture is smooth and glossy.

Using a large metal spoon, add the mixed fruit to the egg mixture and fold in until all the fruit is evenly distributed. Spoon the mixture into the prepared tin. Press down well and smooth the top with the back of a metal spoon. (If desired, the cake may be covered with cling film, stored in a cool place and baked the next day.)

Bake in the centre of a preheated cool oven. Test the first three cake sizes after 2½ hours. If the cake is cooked, it should be evenly risen and will have begun to shrink from the side of the tin. When gently pressed with the fingers, it should spring back. If not cooked, return to the oven and test again at 30 minute intervals. Test the remaining cake sizes after 3 hours. When the cake is cooked, remove from the oven and allow to cool in the tin.

When the cake is cold, remove from the tin, but do not remove the paper as this keeps the cake moist during storage. Spoon several spoonsful of brandy, sherry or rum over the surface of the cake to increase the storage time and to keep the cake moist. Wrap the cake in foil and invert. Store in a cool place. Make Rich fruit cakes at least 2 months in advance to allow the flavour to develop.

Note: If possible, bake only one cake at a time. If any cakes must be cooked together, allow extra cooking time. If a different sized or shaped tin is used, check the quantity of mixture required by comparing it with round or square tins. Fill the round or square tin with water to give a 5 cm (2 inch) depth, then pour the water into the other tin. Check the depth of the water and calculate the amount of cake mixture required, remembering that the volume of mixture must increase.

Rich fruit cake mixture can be baked in various sized and shaped cake tins. The scaled recipe makes sure that they are all the same depth.

This is particularly important for wedding cakes.
Shown here are a 25 cm (10 inch) horseshoe-shaped cake, an 18 cm (7 inch) square cake, and a 20 cm (8 inch) round cake.

Quick mix cake

Metric

Quantity of mixture	Soft margarine, chilled	Caster sugar	Eggs	Self-raising flour	Baking powder	Flavourings (choose one of the following)	Baking tin(s)	Cooking times
100 g	100 g	100 g	2	100 g	1 × 5 ml spoon	4 drops of vanilla essence 4 × 5 ml spoons cocoa powder 2 × 5 ml spoons grated orange or lemon rind 2 × 5 ml spoons instant coffee powder	2 × 18 cm sandwich tins ★18 paper cake cases or tartlet tins 20 cm sandwich tin 20 cm ring mould 18 cm square tin ★900 ml pudding basin ★2 × 1.2 litre pudding basins (each half full)	25 to 30 mins. 15 to 20 mins. 35 to 40 mins. 35 to 40 mins. 35 to 40 mins. 1 hour 10 mins. to 1¼ hours. 55 minutes
175 g	175 g	175 g	3	175 g	1½ × 5 ml spoons	6 drops of vanilla essence 2 × 15 ml spoons cocoa powder 1 × 15 ml spoon grated orange or lemon rind 1 × 15 ml spoon instant coffee powder	8 × 18 × 3.5 cm deep tin	35 to 40 mins.

★*Add 25 g cornflour with the flour. Replace this cornflour with cocoa powder for chocolate-flavoured cake.*

Imperial

Quantity of mixture	Soft margarine, chilled	Caster sugar	Eggs	Self-raising flour	Baking powder	Flavourings (choose one of the following)	Baking tin(s)	Cooking times
4 oz	4 oz	4 oz	2	4 oz	1 teaspoon	4 drops of vanilla essence 4 teaspoons cocoa powder 2 teaspoons grated orange or lemon rind 2 teaspoons instant coffee powder	2 × 7 inch sandwich tins ★18 paper cake cases or tartlet tins 8 inch sandwich tin 8 inch ring mould 7 inch square tin ★1½ pint pudding basin ★2 × 2 pint pudding basins	25 to 30 mins. 15 to 20 mins. 35 to 40 mins. 35 to 40 mins. 35 to 40 mins. 1 hour 10 mins. to 1¼ hours. 55 minutes
6 oz	6 oz	6 oz	3	6 oz	1½ teaspoons	6 drops of vanilla essence 2 tablespoons cocoa powder 1 tablespoon grated orange or lemon rind 1 tablespoon instant coffee powder	11 × 7 × 1½ inch deep tin	35 to 40 mins.

★*Add 1 oz cornflour with the flour. Replace this cornflour with cocoa for chocolate-flavoured cake.*

Quick mix cake mixture can be used for most decorated cakes. Flavour it in various ways and bake it in different tins.
Shown here: two 18 cm (7 inch) sandwich cakes made from 100 g (4 oz) quantity batter; a 175 g (6 oz) quantity batter baked in 900 and 300 ml (1½ and ½ pint) pudding basins for a novelty cake; 175 g (6 oz) quantity batter baked in a 28 × 18 × 3.5 cm (11 × 7 × 1½ inch) oblong tin; 100 g (4 oz) quantity batter baked in an 18 cm (7 inch) square tin; 100 g (4 oz) quantity batter baked in a 20 cm (8 inch) ring mould; and some small cakes

Cooking time: see ingredients
Oven: 160°C, 325°F, Gas Mark 3

Brush the baking tin(s) with melted lard or oil. Line the bases with greaseproof paper and grease the paper. Put the margarine, caster sugar, eggs, sifted flour, baking powder and flavouring, if used, into a mixing bowl. Mix together with a wooden spoon, then beat for 1 to 2 minutes or until the mixture is smooth and glossy. Place into the prepared tin(s) and level the top with the back of a metal spoon.
Bake in the centre of a preheated cool oven for the recommended time (see chart). Test the cake by pressing with the fingertips: if cooked, the cake will spring back and have just begun to shrink from the sides of the tin.
Loosen the edges with a small palette knife and turn out onto a cooling rack. Remove the paper and invert the cake, unless cooked in a ring mould or basin. Leave to cool.

Whisked sponge cake

Metric

Quantity of mixture	Eggs	Caster sugar	Plain flour	Baking powder	Baking tin(s)	Oven temperatures	Cooking times
2-egg	2	50 g	50 g	1 × 2.5 ml spoon	2 × 18 cm sandwich tins	180°C, Gas Mark 4	20 to 25 mins.
					1 × 20 cm sandwich tin	180°C, Gas Mark 4	25 to 30 mins.
					1 × 18 cm square tin	180°C, Gas Mark 4	25 to 30 mins.
					28 × 18 cm Swiss Roll tin	190°C, Gas Mark 5	10 to 12 mins.
					18 sponge drops	190°C, Gas Mark 5	5 to 8 mins.
3-egg	3	75 g	75 g	1 × 2.5 ml spoon	28 × 18 × 3 cm deep tin	180°C, Gas Mark 4	30 to 35 mins.
					20 cm round cake tin	180°C, Gas Mark 4	30 to 35 mins.
					2 × 20 cm sandwich tins	180°C, Gas Mark 4	20 to 25 mins.

Imperial

Quantity of mixture	Eggs	Caster sugar	Plain flour	Baking powder	Baking tin(s)	Oven temperatures	Cooking times
2-egg	2	2 oz	2 oz	½ teaspoon	2 × 7 inch sandwich tins	350°F, Gas Mark 4	20 to 25 mins.
					1 × 8 inch sandwich tin	350°F, Gas Mark 4	25 to 30 mins.
					1 × 7 inch square tin	350°F, Gas Mark 4	25 to 30 mins.
					11 × 7 inch Swiss Roll tin	375°F, Gas Mark 5	10 to 12 mins.
					18 sponge drops	375°F, Gas Mark 5	5 to 8 mins.
3-egg	3	3 oz	3 oz	½ teaspoon	11 × 7 × 1½ inch deep tin	350°F, Gas Mark 4	30 to 35 mins.
					8 inch round cake tin	350°F, Gas Mark 4	30 to 35 mins.
					2 × 8 inch sandwich tins	350°F, Gas Mark 4	20 to 25 mins.

Brush the baking tin(s) with melted lard or oil. Line the bases and sides with greaseproof paper and grease the paper. Put the eggs and sugar in a heatproof bowl over a saucepan of hot but not boiling water. Whisk until the mixture becomes thick and leaves a trail when the whisk is lifted. Remove the bowl from the saucepan and continue to whisk until the mixture becomes cool.

Sift the flour and baking powder over the surface of the mixture. Using a metal spoon, fold in until all the flour has been incorporated. Pour into the prepared tin(s) and shake gently to level the top.

Bake in the centre of a preheated oven for the recommended time (see chart). Test by pressing with the fingertips: if cooked, the cake will spring back and have begun to shrink from the side of the tin. Turn out onto a cooling rack. Remove the paper and invert the cake(s). Leave to cool completely.

For a Swiss roll: cut a piece of greaseproof paper about 2.5 cm (1 inch) larger than the tin and sprinkle thickly with caster sugar. Invert the cake onto the sugared paper. Peel off the greaseproof paper quickly and trim the edges of the cake with a sharp knife. Fold the top short edge in about 2.5 cm (1 inch), then roll the cake up towards you loosely, with the paper inside. Leave for a few minutes to set and cool, then remove the paper. Fill with cream or icing. To fill with jam, spread on the hot cake and roll without the paper.

Variation:
To make a Chocolate whisked sponge cake, replace 2 × 15 ml spoons (2 tablespoons) flour with cocoa for a 2-egg quantity and 3 × 15 ml spoons (3 tablespoons) for a 3-egg quantity.

Vanilla torten sponge cake

Metric	Imperial
4 eggs, separated	4 eggs, separated
125 g caster sugar	4 oz caster sugar
125 g self-raising flour	4 oz self-raising flour
2 × 15 ml spoons corn oil	2 tablespoons corn oil
3 × 15 ml spoons boiling water	3 tablespoons boiling water
1 × 5 ml spoon vanilla essence	1 teaspoon vanilla essence

Cooking time: 50–60 minutes
Oven: 180°C, 350°F, Gas Mark 4

This sponge cake is light, yet firm enough to cut into layers. Use it for special gâteaux.

Brush a deep 20 cm (8 inch) round cake tin with oil. Line the base and side with greaseproof paper and oil the paper. Put the egg yolks, sugar, flour, oil, water and vanilla essence in a bowl and mix together with a wooden spoon. Beat for 1 to 2 minutes or until the batter is smooth. Whisk the egg whites until stiff. Give the batter another stir, then add the whites. Fold in with a metal spoon, gently cutting through the mixture until all the whites have been incorporated. Pour into the prepared tin and bake in the centre of a preheated moderate oven. Test by pressing with the fingertips: if cooked, the cake will spring back and have begun to shrink from the side of the tin.

Lift the cake carefully out of the tin and leave to cool in the paper on a wire rack. The cake will shrink on cooling. Remove the paper when the cake is almost cold.

Makes one 20 cm (8 inch) cake

Variation:
To make a Chocolate torten, replace 25 g (1 oz) of the flour with 25 g (1 oz) cocoa and add 1 × 5 ml spoon (1 teaspoon) baking powder. Dissolve the cocoa in the boiling water, then add it to the egg yolk mixture.

Top right: Beat the egg yolks, sugar, flour, oil and water together
Middle right: Whisk the egg whites until stiff
Right: Use this light, firm sponge cake for layered gâteaux

Left: Use the Whisked sponge cake mixture for gâteaux, especially those decorated with fresh fruit and cream. Shown here: a 2-egg quantity batter baked in a 28 × 18 cm (11 × 7 inch) tin to make a Swiss roll; a 3-egg quantity batter baked in a 28 × 18 × 3.5 cm (11 × 7 × 1½ inch) cake tin, cut in shapes for small cakes; a 2-egg quantity batter baked in two 18 cm (7 inch) sandwich cake tins; a 3-egg quantity chocolate-flavoured batter baked in a 20 cm (8 inch) round deep cake tin; and drop sponge cakes made from a 2-egg quantity

MAKING DECORATIONS

Moulded cake decorations

Make individual cake decorations from bought or homemade Almond paste (see page 32) or Moulding, Satin or Gelatine icing (see pages 16–17).

To colour the Almond paste or icings: Use food colouring. Mix colours to obtain the right shades. Use a skewer to transfer the colouring from the bottle to the icing. Knead the colour into the icing until it is evenly coloured. If a deep colour is required and the colouring makes the icing too soft, add a little icing sugar with the colouring. For a deep colour use concentrated colourings obtainable from specialist cake icing centres (see inside back cover). If the colours are too bright, add a little brown colouring or the flavourless caramel sold for gravy browning. Paint the decorations with food colourings using a fine paint brush; dilute them with egg white, if necessary.

Making animals: Mould in sections as shown below. Use a cocktail stick to press the sections together and stick with egg white, if necessary.

Making flowers: Mould in sections as shown top right. Dip your fingers in cornflour before pressing out pieces of icing. Curve the petals with a paint brush. To make leaves, mould the leaf shape, mark the veins with a knife and leave to dry over a pencil to form a curve.

Making fruit and vegetables: Use cloves or angelica for the stalk ends of the fruits and green icing for the vegetables. Mould the green vegetables in a similar way to flowers. Paint the fruits and vegetables with food colourings.

To store moulded decorations: Place in a box in layers with white tissue in between each layer. Store for up to 2 months.

Above: Elephant, chick, cat, mouse, rabbit
Opposite page, above: Narcissus, violet, Christmas rose, rose, winter jasmin
Opposite page, below: Oranges, pears, lemons, apples, plums, bananas, cherries, grapes

Sugar-frosted flowers, leaves and fruit

Small spring flowers, heathers, roses and leaves of herbs are best for frosting, as are apples, pears, grapes and plums.

Put 1 egg white in a small bowl with 2 × 5 ml spoons (2 teaspoons) water and whisk together with a fork until just mixed. Place a sheet of greaseproof paper on a wire rack.

Dry flower heads and leaves with kitchen paper; wash and dry fruit. Using a fine paint brush, brush flower heads and leaves with the egg white mixture, making sure they are evenly but not thickly coated. Sprinkle with caster sugar and place on the paper to dry. Use the same process for fruits, first dividing grapes into small clusters.

Arrange frosted fruits, flowers and leaves in an attractive arrangement for a centrepiece. Use flowers, leaves and small fruits for decorating cakes and gâteaux. Layer in a box with tissue paper and store for up to 4 weeks.

Chocolate rose leaves

Melt chocolate-flavoured cake covering in a heatproof bowl over a saucepan of hot, not boiling, water. Wash and dry rose leaves. Using a fine paint brush, coat the underside of each leaf with the chocolate covering. Place the leaves, chocolate side uppermost, on a plate and put in the refrigerator to set.

When the chocolate is hard, peel off the rose leaves. Keep the chocolate leaves in small containers in the refrigerator, and use to decorate gâteaux and cakes.

Chocolate curls

Make these from the flat side of a bar of chocolate-flavoured cake covering. Hold a straight-bladed knife at the point and at the handle and place across the chocolate at an angle of about 45°. Draw the knife towards you, carefully shaving off a curl of chocolate. Take care not to cut deeply or the chocolate will not curl. Place the curls on a plate and leave to harden in the refrigerator. Store in a small container until required. Use to decorate cakes and gâteaux.

Chocolate cut-outs

Melt 50 g (2 oz) chocolate-flavoured cake covering and spread thinly onto a piece of foil. Pick up the corners of the foil and drop gently onto a work surface to level the chocolate. Leave the chocolate until just set.

To make chocolate triangles, moons and petals, use a 3.5 cm (1½ inch) and a 2.5 cm (1 inch) plain cutter to cut out chocolate circles. Cut larger circles into 4 triangles with a sharp knife. Using the small cutter, cut each remaining circle in half to form a moon and a petal shape. Place on a plate and leave in the refrigerator to harden. Store in a small container until required, then use to decorate cakes and gâteaux. To keep the shapes shiny, handle as little as possible.

Chocolate squares and triangles

Draw a 15 cm (6 inch) square on a piece of foil and place on a flat board. Melt 50 g (2 oz) chocolate-flavoured cake covering and spread thinly within the marked square. Pick up the corners of the foil and drop onto a work surface to level the chocolate. Leave the chocolate until just set.

Using a ruler and a sharp knife, trim the chocolate to the marked square and cut into nine 5 cm (2 inch) squares. Cut the squares in halves to make triangles. Place on a plate and leave to harden in the refrigerator. Store in small containers until required and use for decorating cakes.

Rose Leaves
Melted chocolate-flavoured covering with rose leaves and paint brush

Paint under the surface of the rose leaves with melted chocolate to coat

Leave chocolate covering to set, then peel off the rose leaf

Curls
Block of chocolate-flavoured cake covering with a straight-bladed knife

Angle the knife to shave off the chocolate into a curl

Finished chocolate curls

1

2

3

Cut-Outs
1. Melted chocolate-flavoured covering spread out thinly on foil
2. Use a cutter to make circles of set chocolate
3. Circles of chocolate covering cut into different shapes

Squares and Triangles
1. Spread melted chocolate-flavoured covering into marked square on foil
2. Cut chocolate into strips, then into squares and triangles

Left: A selection of sugar-frosted flowers, leaves and fruit

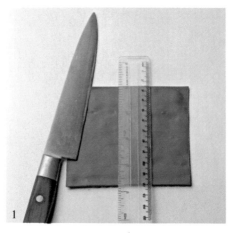

1

2

27

Christmas decorations

Use Moulding icing, Satin icing or Almond paste to make these Christmas novelties. Colour the icing evenly. For the deep colours, mix some icing sugar with the colouring and add it as a paste. Concentrated colourings, available from specialist cake icing centres, are the most successful, especially when Christmas red is required.

Father Christmas: Mould the hat, body and arms from red icing. Make the head, hands and features from flesh-coloured icing. Make the white beard and trimmings for body, hat and sleeves. Assemble the pieces and stick together using a little egg white. Use a fine paint brush to paint the eyes. Make the sack from brown icing and mark a pattern with the back of a knife. Mould various shaped parcels from coloured icing and use contrasting icing for string.

Angel: Make a round flat halo, wing shapes and a flame for the candle from yellow icing. Mould a flesh-coloured head and hands. Mould the body, arms and candle from white icing. Assemble and stick together using egg white. Paint the features with food colourings.

Choir boy: Mould hat and body sleeves from blue icing. Make a flesh-coloured head and hands. Make ruff, cuffs and hymn sheet from white icing. Assemble the pieces and stick together using a little egg white. Paint the features with food colourings.

Clown: Mould a hat, body and arms from yellow icing. Make bobbles for the hat and body, the frill, cuffs, nose and mouth from red icing. Mould the head and hands from flesh-coloured icing. Make two eyes from white icing and paint with brown food colouring. Assemble the pieces and stick together with a little egg white.

Snowman: Mould hat, scarf and buttons from blue icing. Make the head and body from white icing. Make features from brown icing. Assemble the pieces and stick together with a little egg white.

Tree: Mould green icing into a tree shape and a trunk from brown icing. Stick the two together.

Holly: Make cardboard template. Cut around the shape on green icing and mould into shape. Mark veins and dry over a pencil to shape.

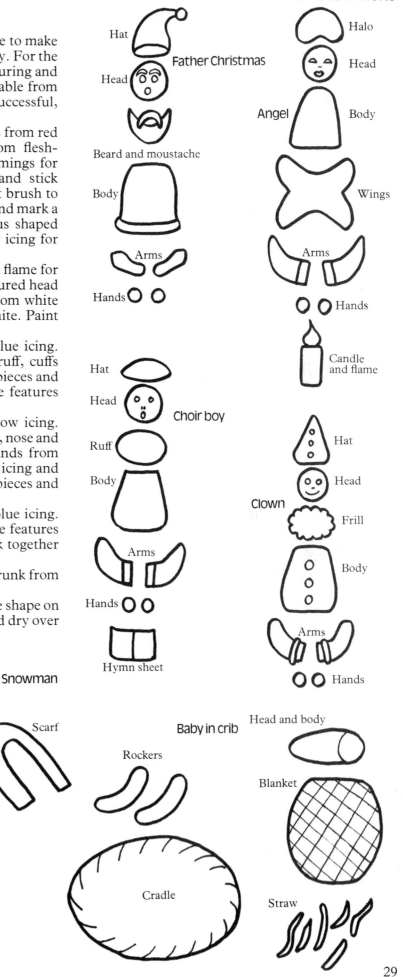

29

Trace the angels and santa in sleigh pictures from the opposite page onto good quality waxed paper or non-stick parchment. Make icing run-outs as described on page 36.

Trace the candle, tree and leaf shapes from the opposite page and cut out in stiff paper. Roll out coloured Almond paste, Moulding icing or Gelatine icing and cut round the shapes with a sharp knife. Mark veins on leaves with a knife. Curl the leaves over a pencil, then leave to dry. Paint the icing leaves with green colouring for a richer colour

Angel

Angel

To make icing pictures to decorate the Christmas cake

Santa in sleigh with reindeer

Christmas tree

Holly leaf

Candles

Ivy leaf

Press the Almond paste under the upturned cake with a palette knife

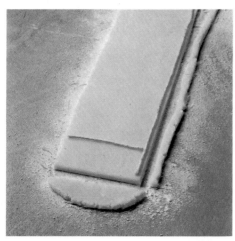

Roll out and trim the Almond paste to size, using the string as a guide

Unroll the coil of Almond paste to cover the side of the cake

ROYAL ICED CAKES

The ultimate in a beautifully iced cake is one covered with Royal icing. It sets very hard and is always used for wedding cakes, where the hardness is necessary for supporting tiers of cakes.

Royal icing is mostly used for a dazzling white finish to the cake which shows off coloured decorations to advantage. A perfect finish can be achieved with care and practice. Intricate designs can be piped in this icing because it has a light, airy texture. Icing pictures that set hard can also be made for decorating cakes.

Almond paste

Metric	Imperial
500 g ground almonds	1 lb ground almonds
250 g icing sugar	8 oz icing sugar
250 g caster sugar	8 oz caster sugar
2 eggs (or 4 yolks)	2 eggs (or 4 yolks)
1 × 2.5 ml spoon almond essence	$\frac{1}{2}$ teaspoon almond essence
1 × 5 ml spoon lemon juice	1 teaspoon lemon juice

Mix the almonds and both sugars together. Beat the eggs or yolks with the almond essence and lemon juice. Stir into the almond mixture and mix to a firm paste. Cover to prevent drying.

Makes 1 kg (2 lb) Almond paste, sufficient to cover the top and side of a 20 cm (8 inch) round or square cake

To cover a cake with Almond paste

Sift some icing sugar over a work surface. Roll out half of the almond paste 2.5 cm (1 inch) larger than the top of the cake, about 2 cm ($\frac{1}{2}$ inch) thick. Brush the top of the cake with boiled, sieved apricot jam. Invert the cake onto the almond paste. Draw up the edge of the almond paste level to the side of the cake using a small palette knife. Press under the cake, then cut off any surplus, keeping the knife pressed against the side of the cake. Return the cake upright and place on a cake board. Brush the side with apricot jam.

Cut two pieces of string, one the exact size of the height of the cake and the other the length around the cake. Roll out the remaining almond paste and trim to the length and width of the string. Roll the almond paste into a coil and place one end on the side of the cake. Unroll carefully around the side of the cake to cover evenly. Using a small palette knife, smooth the top and side joins.

Follow the same method to cover a square cake, but cut four oblongs to fit each side of the cake. Press these onto the sides gently and smooth the joins with a small palette knife. Leave the covered cake in a warm dry room until the surface feels dry and firm, overnight for most cakes. For wedding cakes that may be stored for over a year, leave the almond paste to dry for 1 week to avoid the oil from the almond paste staining the Royal icing.

Royal icing

Metric	Imperial
2–3 × 5 ml spoons powdered egg albumen	*2–3 teaspoons powdered egg albumen*
4 × 15 ml spoons water	*4 tablespoons water*
500 g icing sugar, sifted	*1 lb icing sugar, sifted*
or	or
2–3 egg whites	*2–3 egg whites*
1 × 5 ml spoon glycerine	*1 teaspoon glycerine*
500 g icing sugar	*1 lb icing sugar*

Place the egg albumen and water in a bowl. Whisk with a fork until well mixed. *Or* place egg whites and glycerine in a bowl and whisk lightly with a fork. Stir in sufficient icing sugar to make the consistency of unwhipped double cream. Beat with a wooden spoon or a whisk, adding small quantities of icing sugar until the mixture has become very white and the icing forms a firm peak on a spoon.

If an electric beater is used to make the icing, keep the machine at the lowest speed and leave the icing for 24 hours before using to remove air bubbles. Before using, stir well with a wooden spoon.

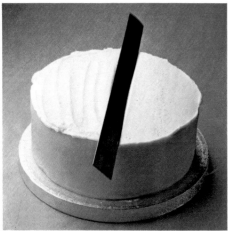

Draw the straight edge across the top of the cake to give a smooth finish

Draw the scraper around the side of the cake to smooth the icing

Cover the icing with a damp cloth during the time it is being used, then store in an airtight container.

The Royal icing used for coating a cake should not be as stiff as for piping. Mix it to a soft peak for coating and a stiff peak for piping.

Make small quantities of icing at a time as there is less risk of the icing becoming spoiled. Glycerine softens the icing, making it easier to cut.

Makes a 500 g (1 lb) quantity of icing

To cover a cake with Royal icing

The top: Place the cake on the board in the centre of the turntable, or on an upturned plate. Place a quantity of icing onto the centre of the cake. With a small palette knife begin to spread the icing over the top surface of the cake using a 'paddling motion'. At the same time keep turning the turntable or moving across the cake if it is on a plate. Remove surplus icing from the top edge of the cake with a palette knife. Clean the knife ready for the next time.

Remove the cake from the turntable. Hold the metal rule at an angle of about 30° and, with a straight and determined movement, draw it towards you across the cake, taking care not to press too much for the first coat. Clean the rule immediately before putting it down.

Hold the blade of the palette knife parallel with the side of the cake and remove surplus icing from the top edge. Leave the top to dry for at least 1 hour before icing the side.

To ice the side: Place the cake on the turntable or upturned plate and spread a small quantity of icing onto the side of the cake. Hold a side-scraper to the side of the cake at a slight angle towards the cake. Pass the other hand under and round the turntable so that a complete revolution can be made. Keeping the scraper in the hand quite still, revolve the turntable quite quickly and smoothly so as to smooth the side in one movement. Draw off the scraper at an angle so the 'take-off' mark is hardly noticeable. Remove the small ridge of icing from the top edge of the cake with a palette knife held at 45° and revolve the turntable in an anti-clockwise direction. This will leave a small bevel where the border can be piped.

Leave the cake to dry overnight in a dry room. Smooth any roughness from the icing with fine glass-paper held over a small wooden block. Use a clean brush to remove the powdered icing. Repeat this method to cover the cake with two more thin coats of icing.

Use a similar method to ice the sides of a square cake. Ice two opposite sides first and leave them to dry for about 1 hour, then repeat icing the remaining sides. Take care to remove the surplus icing from the top edge and corners of the cake as each side is iced, forming sharp corners and edges.

Icing the cake board: When the cake has been completely iced, coat the cake board with a thin layer of icing. Hold the side-scraper at an angle on the icing and turn the turntable one revolution to smooth the surface. Remove surplus icing on the edge of the cake board with a palette knife. The same applies with a square cake, but coat two opposite sides of the cake board, then leave for 1 hour before coating the two remaining sides. Cover the board with two coats of icing.

Piping designs

Versatile Royal icing can be fashioned into many designs from messages to fragile-looking roses. Most designs are made with writing and star tubes. The small tubes need fairly soft icing, the large tubes, stiffer icing. Keep the bowl of icing covered with a clean damp cloth or a plastic lid during use to prevent drying; lumps in the icing would be disastrous. The icing must be beaten well to form peaks and to avoid breaks; over-beating (as when a mixer is used) forms air pockets which also cause breaks.

Using a plain tube

Straight lines: For straight lines or curves, press the icing onto the surface at the start, then lift up the tube, press out a thread of icing, let it fall onto the surface and guide it into the correct place. Bring the tube down at the end of the line, pressing it gently onto the surface to break the thread. Neaten the ends with a hat pin. Avoid thick beads of icing at each end.

An effective decoration can be achieved by starting the design with a thick plain tube, such as a No. 4, then over-piping with finer icing lines or curves, finishing with a row of beads (see pages 42–43).

Beads: Hold the tube upright but not quite touching the cake. Press out the icing to form the required size of bead, press down, then pull off sharply to form a point. Beads of graduated size look attractive. Use them also for over-piping lines or for the edges of cakes and boards.

Trellis: Pipe straight parallel lines. Leave to dry for about 20 minutes, then repeat in an opposite direction, either to make diamonds or squares. Up to four layers may be built up. It is easy to remove a line that has fallen in the wrong place if the layer below it is dry.

Scrolls: Make curves of icing, lifting the tube to achieve an attractive curve. Use for the sides or the tops of cakes. With practice it is possible to graduate the thickness of the scroll.

Scribbling: This is one of the quickest and most effective ways of adding texture to Royal icing, and it is useful for disguising a less than perfect surface. Hold the tube upright touching the surface and move the tube continuously in different directions in a circular movement to make loops of icing.

Writing: If coloured icing is required, either paint the design or over-pipe white icing with the colour. Piping directly onto the cake in colour does not allow for mistakes because the coloured piping would stain the surface icing. Prick out the design or trace it in pencil. Make sure it is on the cake in the right position. Make each stroke separately, finish off neatly and join up the next stroke.

Straight lines

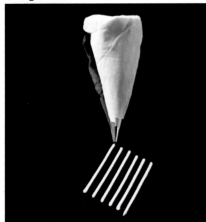

Beads

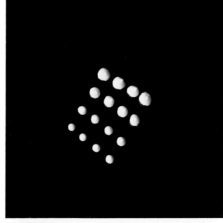

Trellis

Scrolls

Scribbling

Writing

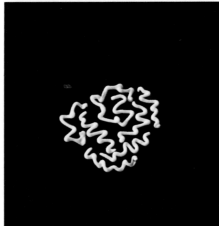

Using a star tube

For large tubes, a nylon piping bag fitted with a collar and a small tube is quickest, but there is not as much control as when using a paper piping bag.

Stars: Hold the tube upright on the surface, press out until the size is achieved, then pull off sharply to form a point.

Shells: Hold the piping bag at an angle. Start in the centre of the shell. Move the tube away from you, then towards you, pressing out the icing over the centre part. Pull off sharply to form a point. Start the next shell just past the point of the first to position the rounded part on its point.

Whirls: Make a circular movement with the tube. Press down when it is of the required size, then pull off sharply to form a point.

Scrolls: Make a circular movement, then pipe a 'tail' and pull off sharply.

Reverse scrolls: Make alternate clockwise and anti-clockwise scrolls, starting each on the point of the 'tail' of the previous scroll.

Coils: Make small circular movements in a clockwise direction.

Roses: Use a special petal tube and stiff Royal icing. Spear a small piece of waxed paper onto a cocktail stick. Hold the tube with the thicker part downwards. Press out the icing onto the paper and twist the cocktail stick to form the centre of the flower. Repeat, building up the petals into a rose shape. Spear the cocktail stick into a potato and leave until the rose is dry.

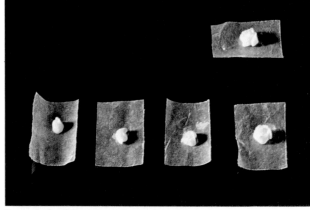

Steps in building up rose petals

Finished rose

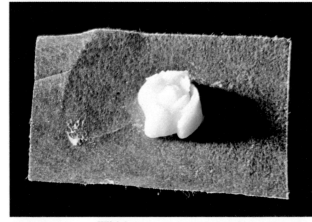

Stars

Shells

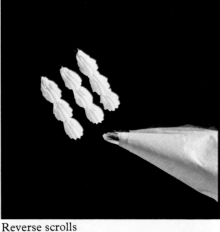

Whirls

Scrolls

Reverse scrolls

Coils

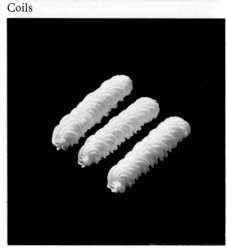

Trace the design onto waxed paper from a book or greetings card

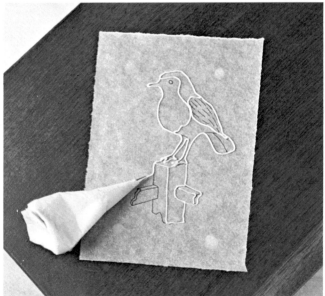

Outline the design using a fine writing tube

Fill with soft icing, the outside first then the centre

36

Icing run-out pictures and shapes

These delicate cake decorations can be made in almost any design. They are particularly useful for making pictures depicting hobbies and club or regimental badges for special celebration cakes. They are made from Royal icing; the shape is outlined by piping and the centre filled with soft Royal icing. The icing can be coloured and painted with food colouring. Run-outs are fragile and it is best to choose solid shapes that will not break easily.

Preparing the design: Trace the design from a picture in a book or on a greetings card onto the underside of waxed paper or onto a piece of greaseproof paper. Place the paper on a level board or a sheet of glass and secure with a dot of Royal icing in each corner. Cover with waxed paper, shiny side uppermost, or non-stick baking parchment and secure with icing. Make more tracings than are required, in case of breakages.

The icing: Make Royal icing: if using egg whites, omit the glycerine or lemon juice, or use egg albumen of double strength. Make the icing of piping consistency for a fine plain tube, that is slightly softer than stiff peak stage. If only one colour is being used, for example for a leaf, colour both the icing for piping and filling in. Use white icing if more than one colour is being used.

For filling the shape, make the icing thinner with egg albumen, egg white or water until of the consistency of double cream. It should coat the back of a spoon and slowly level itself when returned to the bowl. Mix gently to avoid air bubbles.

Making the run-out: Have ready sufficient piping bags, one for outlining the design and others for filling in with each colour. Use the stiff icing for outlining and a No. 1 writing tube. Fill the other bags with each colour of soft icing; no tube is required. Have ready a cocktail stick or a paint brush. Large pieces can be filled with a teaspoon.

Pipe the outline of the design, making sure there are no breaks and that the corners are closed (use a hat pin to neaten the corners). Snip the point off a bag of soft icing and fill in the design, going round the outside first before the icing has dried. Fill the design completely, using a cocktail stick or a paint brush to spread the icing, if necessary. The icing should be level and slightly rounded. Prick out any air bubbles with the paint brush or hat pin. Leave the run-outs in a warm dry room, near a fan heater or radiator to set the surface quickly, then leave to dry for about 12 hours for small pieces, 24 hours for large pieces. In damp weather up to 3 days, covered with soft tissue, may be necessary. Over-pipe or colour the run-out when quite dry.

To remove the paper: Place the run-out on a thick book, slightly over the edge. Pull down the paper, then turn the run-out until all the edges are loose. Gently pull off the rest of the paper, supporting the run-out with the fingers.

To store: Leave on the waxed paper and store in an airtight tin in between layers of soft white tissue for up to 6 months.

Far right: Here are some ideas for templates for icing run-out pictures

Prick out any bubbles with a hat pin

Over-pipe the design

Peel the paper off the design if being used straight away

Candle in holder

Hearts

Bell with bow

Sailboat

Numbers

37

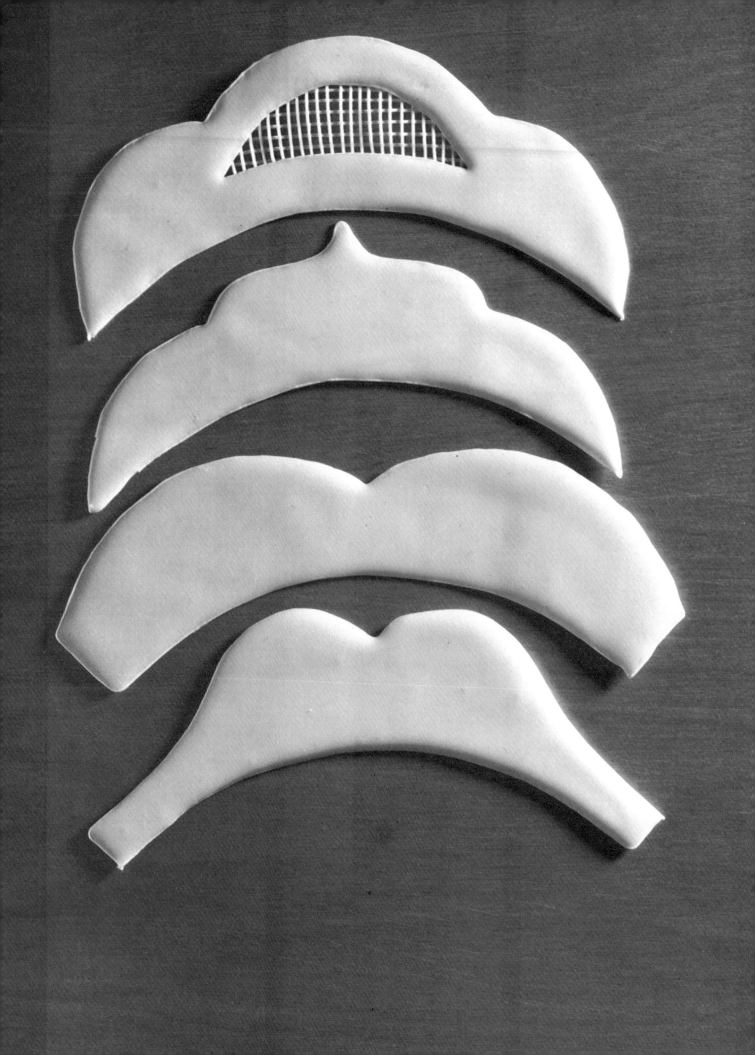

Run-out icing collars

The method for making run-out pictures described on pages 36–37 can be extended to make collars for the cakes. These fine sheets of icing give a cake a very smart professional look (see pages 48–49). The design is raised above the surface of the cake with a thick rope of icing. Two layers can be made, but this should not be attempted by beginners. A round or square collar can be made, but removing it from the paper is often very difficult. Start by making a collar in four sections.

Trace one of the designs below and make four sections (plus an extra one in case of breakage) to fit the top of the cake. Take the exact measurement from the top of the cake. Make the run-out collar on non-stick baking parchment; it does not wrinkle like waxed paper. Leave the collar sections to dry for up to 3 days, then over-pipe, if necessary, and carefully remove from the parchment. A beaded edge looks attractive and covers any roughness of the edge.

To make the trellis insert, place the icing sections upside-down on clean paper. Pipe threads of icing from a No. 1 tube across the width, then in the opposite direction. Leave to dry.

Decorating the cake board: The cake board should be larger than the overlapping collar, or it will look unbalanced. A 20 cm (8 inch) cake needs a 30 cm (12 inch) board. Repeat the collar design on the board. Outline and fill in in a similar way.

Wedding cakes

A sparkling white royal iced cake is the traditional wedding cake, although colour can be introduced in the decoration to match the bride's dress or flowers. A one, two or three tiered cake can be made depending on the number of portions required. The cake can be round, square or horseshoe-shaped. It is usual to have 5 cm (2 inches) difference in the size of each tier. A very firm, rich fruit cake is best because it is usual to cut 2.5 cm (1 inch) squares of cake. Make the cake 6 months in advance to give it a chance to mature. Cover it with Almond paste and leave to dry for one week, if it is anticipated that a tier of the cake may be kept for a year (it is often saved to celebrate the first wedding anniversary). For an easy-to-cut icing, add 1×5 ml spoon (1 teaspoon) glycerine to the icing for the bottom tier, 2×5 ml spoons (2 teaspoons) for the middle tier and 3×5 ml spoons (3 teaspoons) glycerine for the top tier. The icing must be really dry before the cakes are supported on the pillars. If there is any doubt, place a small silver cake card in the centre of the cake before placing the pillars in position. Hire a cake stand and knife from a local confectioner.

To cut the cake: After the ceremonial cake cutting by the bride and groom, the cake is always cut in half, then in 2.5 cm (1 inch) pieces. This method makes it easy to calculate the number of servings. For example, a 20 cm (8 inch) square cake will cut into 60 slices (there is wastage on each corner); a 20 cm (8 inch) round cake will cut into 44 slices. A square cake is easy to calculate, and a round cake will yield about two-thirds the number of slices.

Left: Run-out icing collars
Below: Templates to trace for two of the collars shown left

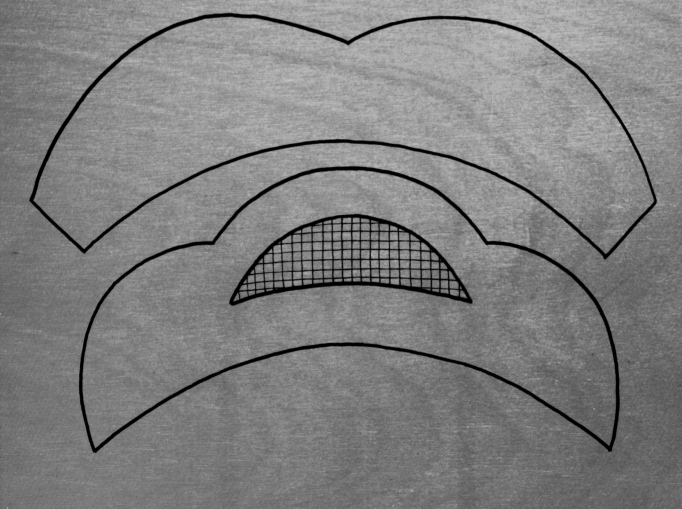

Good luck wedding cake

Metric	Imperial·
1½ quantity Almond Paste (see page 32)	1¼ quantity Almond Paste (see page 32)
1 × 25 cm round quantity Rich Fruit Cake mixture, baked in a 25 cm horse-shoe cake tin (see pages 18–19)	1 × 10 inch round quantity Rich Fruit Cake mixture, baked in a 10 inch horseshoe cake tin (see pages 18–19)
Apricot jam, boiled and sieved	Apricot jam, boiled and sieved
1 × 30 cm round silver cake board	1 × 12 inch round silver cake board
Royal Icing, made with 1.5 kg icing sugar (see page 33)	Royal Icing, made with 3 lb icing sugar (see page 33)

Decoration:
5 large horseshoe-shaped icing run-outs (see pages 36–37)
12 small horseshoe-shaped icing run-outs (see pages 36–37)
Blue food colouring
20 small silver leaves
1 metre 1-cm wide silver cake board edging

Decoration:
5 large horseshoe-shaped icing run-outs (see pages 36–37)
12 small horseshoe-shaped icing run-outs (see pages 36–37)
Blue food colouring
20 small silver leaves
1¼ yards ½-inch wide silver cake board edging

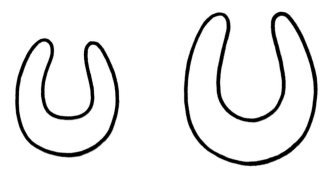

Use these templates to make the horseshoe-shaped run-outs to decorate the cake

Roll half the Almond paste into a horseshoe shape. Brush the cake with apricot jam, then place the cake on top of the paste. Trim to fit. Place the cake carefully on the cake board. Do not move again as this shape can break easily. Roll out and trim the remaining Almond paste to fit outside and inside the horseshoe. Press onto the cake, then smooth all joins with a small palette knife and leave until dry.

With the two ends facing, cover the cake with Royal icing. Start to pull the straight edge across from the rounded part of horseshoe and finish at the two ends. Remove surplus icing carefully with a palette knife. When the top is dry, coat the outside edge as for a round cake, then cover the inside edge, but use a small palette knife instead of a side scraper. Finally ice the two ends of the horseshoe. Dry and repeat to give three coats of icing.

Ice the cake board as for a round cake, covering the board evenly just to the opening of the two ends. Dilute a little icing with egg albumen or egg white until the icing just coats the back of a spoon. Pour the icing into the centre of the horseshoe to coat the board evenly and leave to dry. Reserve the remaining icing for decoration.

Colour a little Royal icing pale blue with a few drops of blue food colouring. Using a greaseproof paper piping bag fitted with a No. 42 small star tube, pipe stars to outline each horseshoe run-out. Leave to dry, then remove the paper carefully from the run-outs.

Using a No. 7 star tube, pipe a coil around the top edges and around the base and ends of the horseshoe.

Secure eight small horseshoe run-outs, evenly spaced apart, around the outside of the cake with a little icing. Place one on each flat end of the cake and two opposite on the inside of the cake, securing with a little icing. Place one large horseshoe run-out in the centre of the inside of the cake, resting the two ends on the cake board.

On the four remaining large horseshoe run-outs, pipe a swirl of icing on the back, at each side of the horseshoes. Arrange two horseshoes at an angle on the centre top of the cake and the remaining two at each side, halfway from the ends and centre. Pipe a star of icing in between each horseshoe on top of the cake and arrange two silver leaves on each icing star.

Using a No. 2 plain piping tube, pipe beads of white icing in a scalloped pattern in between the horseshoes on the outside and ends of cake. Using the No. 2 piping tube, pipe blue beads of icing on top of the white beads. Pipe three blue beads of icing onto the stars on top of the cake which secure the silver leaves. Arrange two silver leaves and three beads of blue icing on the front corners of the cake and the remaining leaves underneath the scalloped beading on the side of the cake. Place the remaining small horseshoe on the centre front of the cake board. Put the silver cake board edging onto the board.

To store an iced wedding cake: If the Almond paste has dried sufficiently, the cake will store in an airtight tin without discoloration for about 2 years. Seal the tin with sticky tape. It is not advisable to freeze an iced cake; the icing will crack.

Wild rose wedding cake

Metric	Imperial
1 × 20 cm square Rich Fruit Cake (see pages 18–19)	*1 × 8 inch square Rich Fruit Cake (see pages 18–19)*
1 × 15 cm square Rich Fruit Cake (see pages 18–19)	*1 × 6 inch square Rich Fruit Cake (see pages 18–19)*
Apricot jam, boiled and sieved	*Apricot jam, boiled and sieved*
Double quantity Almond Paste (see page 32)	*Double quantity Almond Paste (see page 32)*
1 × 25 cm and 1 × 20 cm silver cake boards	*1 × 10 inch and 1 × 8 inch silver cake boards*
Royal Icing, made with 2 kg icing sugar (see page 33)	*Royal Icing, made with 4 lb icing sugar (see page 33)*

Decoration:
Pink food colouring
4 small silver horseshoes
4 large silver horseshoes
1.5 metres 1.25-cm wide silver braid
8 small moulded wild roses (see pages 24–25)
6 medium moulded wild roses (see pages 24–25)
4 large moulded wild roses (see pages 24–25)
Fern
4 cake pillars
Mimosa

Decoration:
Pink food colouring
4 small silver horseshoes
4 large silver horseshoes
1¾ yards ½-inch wide silver braid
8 small moulded wild roses (see pages 24–25)
6 medium moulded wild roses (see pages 24–25)
4 large moulded wild roses (see pages 24–25)
Fern
4 cake pillars
Mimosa

Cover the cakes with apricot jam and then Almond paste and place them on the cake boards. Leave to dry for up to 1 week, then cover them with three thin coats of Royal icing (reserve the remaining icing for decoration).

To decorate the cakes, make a template for the design as shown below. Take the exact size of the cake and calculate the measurements of the template from the outside. Cut out a template for each cake; place on top of the cakes and prick round.

Place the scroll design from the following page onto greaseproof paper (adjust the size, if necessary; the ends of the scroll should be 2.5 cm (1 inch) from the corners). Reverse the paper, place it against the side of the cake in the centre and trace over the design with a pencil to mark it on the cake faintly in pencil. Repeat on each side, reversing the paper.

Fit a paper piping bag with a No. 2 plain piping tube and fill with Royal icing. Outline the design. Use the pin to improve the points of the design. Repeat, building up a second layer on top of the first with the No. 2 tube. Pipe curved lines next to the first lines then rows of beads.

Pipe over the scroll design on each side, then over-pipe with beads (if you find the plain piping difficult just pipe the beads over the marked scroll). Pipe graduated beads from the centre of each scroll design to the top and bottom edges and on each corner.

Fit a paper piping bag with a No. 8 star tube and pipe shells around the top and bottom edges of each cake. Start at each corner and work towards the centre bead.

Put about 4 × 15 ml spoons (4 tablespoons) icing in a small bowl and tint pale pink with food colouring. Fit a greaseproof paper piping bag with a No. 2 plain tube and fill with the pink icing. Pipe a pink bead on the side of the cakes between each shell on the base. Pipe small loops to outline each shell on the cake boards. Pipe a row of beads on the edge of each cake board.

Pipe a little icing on one corner of the small board and place a small silver horseshoe upright on it. Support it by placing a soft ball of paper tissue behind the horseshoe. Repeat on each corner then on the large board with the large horseshoes. Remove the paper after 30 minutes.

Cut the silver braid to fit each cake board and secure with a little icing.

Make the wild roses as described for Christmas roses on pages 24–25 with pink petals and yellow centres. Place groups of two small moulded wild roses with some fern in each corner of the small cake; secure with a little icing. Repeat with the medium-sized flowers on the large cake.

Place the cake pillars in the centre of the large cake and place the small cake centrally on the pillars. Decorate the centre of the cake around the pillars with large and medium moulded wild roses and fern. Place a silver vase of mimosa and moulded wild roses on top of the cake.

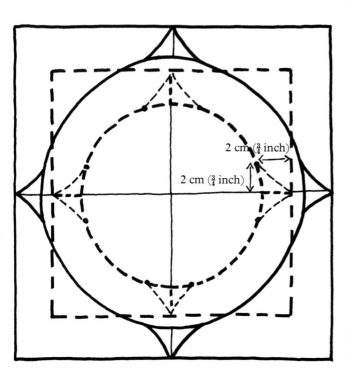

2 cm (¾ inch)

2 cm (¾ inch)

Use this design to make templates for decorating the tops of the two cake tiers. The solid line is for the 20 cm (8 inch) cake and the dotted line for the 15 cm (6 inch) cake. Overleaf is the template for the scroll design used on the sides of the cake tiers

Use this scroll design to decorate the sides of the Wild rose wedding cake on pages 42–43. (The solid line is for the 20 cm (8 inch) cake and the dotted line for the 15 cm (6 inch) cake.) Transfer the design with pencil to greaseproof paper, then reverse the paper and hold it against the side of the cake. Trace over the design so that a faint pencil line is left on the cake icing

Template diagram for top of Rosebud wedding cake

3 cm
(1¼ inch)

The Rosebud wedding cake on pages 46–47 has three tiers decorated using this template design. Cut out a 25 cm (10 inch) circle for the template for the largest cake tier. Mark and cut out as shown. Repeat with a 20 cm (8 inch) circle, marking a 2.5 cm (1 inch) line, and a 15 cm (6 inch) circle, marking a 1 cm (¾ inch) line

The diagram below shows the template folded into a cone-shape. This is used to make a scallop shape on the side of each cake layer

3 cm
(1¼ inch)

Fold

Fold

Rosebud wedding cake

Metric	Imperial
1 × 15 cm round Rich Fruit Cake (see pages 18–19)	1 × 6 inch round Rich Fruit Cake (see pages 18–19)
1 × 20 cm round Rich Fruit Cake (see pages 18–19)	1 × 8 inch round Rich Fruit Cake (see pages 18–19)
1 × 25 cm round Rich Fruit Cake (see pages 18–19)	1 × 10 inch round Rich Fruit Cake (see pages 18–19)
Apricot jam, boiled and sieved	Apricot jam, boiled and sieved
Triple quantity Almond Paste (see page 32)	Triple quantity Almond Paste (see page 32)
1 × 20 cm round silver cake board	1 × 8 inch round silver cake board
1 × 25 cm round silver cake board	1 × 10 inch round silver cake board
1 × 30 cm round silver cake board	1 × 12 inch round silver cake board
Royal Icing, made with 2.75 kg icing sugar (see page 33)	Royal Icing, made with 6 lb icing sugar (see page 33)

Decoration:	Decoration:
½ quantity Moulding Icing (see page 17)	½ quantity Moulding Icing (see page 17)
Salmon pink or red and yellow food colouring	Salmon pink or red and yellow food colouring
2.5 metres 1-cm wide silver cake board edging	2½ yards ½-inch wide silver cake board edging
8 × 7.5-cm high cake pillars	8 × 3-inch high cake pillars
A small silver vase of flowers	A small silver vase of flowers

Make templates for decorating the tops of the cake tiers as shown on the previous page

Cover the cakes with apricot jam and then Almond paste and place on the cake boards. Cover each cake with three coats of Royal icing; reserve the remaining icing for decoration.

Colour the Moulding icing apricot pink with salmon pink food colouring or red and yellow colouring. Make 18 roses and 36 rose buds (see pages 24–25).

Place the 25 cm (10 inch) template on top of the large cake. Using a hat pin or needle, prick along the scalloped line onto the cake surfaces. Remove the template.

Fold the template into the original cone shape and use the scallop shape to mark the side of the cake. Fold the point of the cone so that the points reach the edge of the cake and the template is against the side of the cake. Match the scallop shape on top of the cake with the template scallop below; prick out the shape. Repeat, moving the template until the scalloped design is marked around the side of the cake. Mark the design on the other cakes using the remaining two templates.

Using a greaseproof paper piping bag fitted with a No. 2 plain tube and Royal icing, pipe a diagonal trellis design within the marked scalloped design.

Using a No. 7 star tube, pipe a row of stars around the scallop edge on the top of each cake, at the edge of the trellis, and a row of stars on the outer edge of the cakes and around the base.

Using a No. 2 plain piping tube, start piping a thread of icing at the beginning of the scallop design on the side of the cake. Once the thread is attached, pipe the icing slightly away from the cake until it covers almost half of the scallop line. Attach it to the cake, then pipe the second half of the scallop and secure to the cake. Repeat around the side of each cake.

In the centre of each scallop on the side of the large cake, use a little Royal icing to secure three rose buds. Repeat, securing two rose buds in the centre of each scallop on the 20 cm (8 inch) cake and one rose bud on the 15 cm (6 inch) cake.

Using a No. 2 plain piping tube, pipe three beads of icing in a triangle each side of the rose buds and at the point of the scallops all around the side of the cake. Repeat on the remaining two cakes.

Colour a little Royal icing apricot pink and, using a No. 2 plain piping tube, pipe apricot pink beads of icing on top of the white beads of icing around the side of the cake and the remaining two cakes.

Half fill a greaseproof paper piping bag with Royal icing. Fold down the top and squeeze the icing to the point. Cut off the point diagonally on the sides to form an inverted 'V'. Pipe leaves at each side and underneath the rose buds and at each side of the apricot pink 'beads' around the sides of the cakes. Secure the remaining roses on the top of the cakes at the point of each scallop. Repeat on the remaining cakes. Pipe leaves at each side of these roses.

With Royal icing, secure the silver edging to the cake boards.

Place four cake pillars in the centre of the large cake and place the medium cake centrally on the pillars. Put the remaining four pillars in the centre of the medium cake and place the small cake centrally on top. Place a small silver vase of flowers on top.

Silver wedding cake

Metric	Imperial
1 × 20 cm round Rich Fruit Cake (see pages 18–19)	1 × 8 inch round Rich Fruit Cake (see pages 18–19)
Apricot jam, boiled and sieved	Apricot jam, boiled and sieved
1 quantity Almond Paste (see page 32)	1 quantity Almond Paste (see page 32)
1 × 30 cm round silver cake board	1 × 12 inch round silver cake board
Double quantity Royal Icing (see page 33)	Double quantity Royal Icing (see page 33)
1 metre 2.5-cm wide silver cake board edging	1 yard 1-inch wide silver cake board edging
4 icing run-out collar sections (see pages 38–39)	4 icing run-out collar sections (see pages 38–39)
8 silver paper leaves	8 silver paper leaves
4 small silver horseshoes	4 small silver horseshoes
1 silver 'Congratulations'	1 silver 'Congratulations'

Cover the cake with apricot jam and then Almond paste. Place on the cake board. Cover the cake and board with three thin layers of Royal icing. (Reserve the remaining icing for decoration.) Fit the silver cake board edging around the side of the cake, and secure with a little Royal icing.

Fit a greaseproof paper piping bag with a No. 7 star tube, fill with Royal icing and pipe a few stars at intervals around the top edge of the cake.

Carefully fit the collar sections in position about 5 mm (¼ inch) in from the edge. Press gently into position. Pipe stars around the inside edge of the collar.

Pipe a triangle of stars on the side of the cake underneath the join of each collar section. Pipe a swirl of icing at each join and place a silver leaf on each.

Place a cut-out template of the collar design on the iced cake board with the centre of the design below the joins of the icing run-outs on the top. Prick out the design with a pin, then repeat around the cake to mark four sections. Outline the design with star piping.

Using a No. 2 plain piping tube, fill in the design with scribbling. Pipe a swirl of icing between each design and place a silver leaf on top, as on the top.

Secure four silver horseshoes on top of the cake in between the leaves with a little icing. Place the 'Congratulations' in the centre of the cake and secure with a little icing. Alternatively, make run-outs of numbers for the appropriate dates or initials as described on page 37.

Golden bell cake

Metric	Imperial
1 × 20 cm square Rich Fruit Cake (see pages 18–19)	1 × 8 inch square Rich Fruit Cake (see pages 18–19)
Apricot jam, boiled and sieved	Apricot jam, boiled and sieved
1 quantity Almond Paste (see page 32)	1 quantity Almond Paste (see page 32)
1 × 25 cm square gold cake board	1 × 10 inch square gold cake board
Double quantity Royal Icing (see page 33)	Double quantity Royal Icing (see page 33)
16 icing run-out bells (see pages 36–37)	16 icing run-out bells (see pages 36–37)
Gold food colouring (see note)	Gold food colouring (see note)
White and gold ribbon bow	White and gold ribbon bow
1 gold '50' emblem	1 gold '50' emblem
1 metre narrow gold ribbon	1 yard narrow gold ribbon

Cover the cake with apricot jam and then Almond paste. Place on the cake board. Cover with three thin layers of Royal icing. Reserve the remaining icing for decoration.

Fill a greaseproof paper piping bag fitted with a No. 2 plain tube with Royal icing and pipe the outline of each run-out bell with beads of icing. When the bells are dry, paint the beads with gold food colouring using a fine paintbrush. Remove the paper from the bells.

Using a No. 8 star tube, pipe a row of shells around the top and bottom edges of the cake.

Using a No. 2 plain tube, pipe a scallop design on the side of the cake underneath the shell design on the top edge. Pipe a bead at the join of each scallop.

Secure two bells on each side of the cake in the centre with a little icing. Pipe five stars at each side and one at each corner between the bells.

Use the No. 2 plain tube to pipe a thread of icing from the centre of each star in a scallop design. Pipe a bead in the centre of each star; paint with gold.

Arrange pairs of bells in each corner on top of the cake and secure with icing. Place a white and gold ribbon bow and a '50' emblem in the centre. Place gold ribbon around the cake board and secure with icing.

Alternatively, make run-outs of numbers as shown on pages 36–37 for decorating the centre, or write the numbers and initials.

Note: Gold food colouring can be obtained from specialist cake icing centres (see inside back cover for the addresses).

Silver wedding cake; Golden bell cake

Coming of age cake

Metric

1 × 20 cm round
quantity Rich Fruit Cake
mixture (see pages 18–19)
1 × 38 cm × 25 cm
cake board or piece of
wood covered with foil
Apricot jam, boiled and
sieved
1 quantity Almond Paste
(see page 32)
1½ quantity Gelatine or
Moulding Icing (see
page 17)
1 quantity Royal Icing
(see page 33)
Pink food colouring
18 or 21 icing number
run-outs (see
pages 36–37)

Imperial

1 × 8 inch round
quantity Rich Fruit Cake
mixture (see pages 18–19)
1 × 15 inch × 10 inch
cake board or piece of
wood covered with foil
Apricot jam, boiled and
sieved
1 quantity Almond Paste
(see page 32)
1½ quantity Gelatine or
Moulding Icing (see
page 17)
1 quantity Royal Icing
(see page 33)
Pink food colouring
18 or 21 icing number
run-outs (see
pages 36–37)

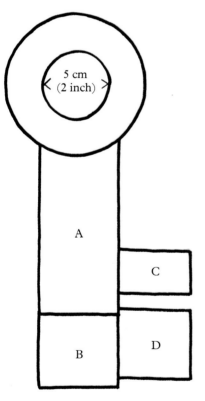

Left: cut the 15 cm (6 inch) square
cake into four pieces as shown and
assemble into the key shape as
above, with the 13 cm (5 inch)
round cake

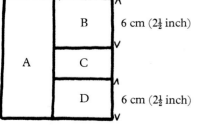

Divide the Rich fruit cake mixture between a 13 cm (5 inch) round cake tin and a 15 cm (6 inch) square tin. Bake according to the instructions in the basic recipe (see pages 18–19), checking the round cake after 2¼ hours. Cool.

Using a 5 cm (2 inch) plain cutter and a small sharp knife, cut a circle out of the centre of the round cake. Remove the circle and place round cake on the cake board.

Cut the square cake in half. Place one half next to the round cake for the 'shaft' of the key. Cut two 6 × 7.5 cm (2½ × 3 inch) pieces from the remaining oblong piece of cake. Place one piece next to the 'shaft' on the cake board and the other piece with the remaining small piece alongside the 'shaft', a little apart. This key shape is now ready for covering with apricot jam and then Almond paste.

Following the instructions on page 32, cover the top of the round cake, using a 5 cm (2 inch) cutter to remove the centre piece from the circle of Almond paste. Place in position on the cake board and cover the outside and inside of the cake. Cover the top of the 'shaft' as one piece and place on the board. Cover all the sides with strips of Almond paste. Press the 'shaft' and circle together. Fill in the edges with Almond paste and shape with the fingers. Take the two remaining pieces of cake and cover with Almond paste. Place on the cake board but do not join to the key shape.

Sprinkle a board with cornflour and roll out two-thirds of the Gelatine or Moulding icing to an oblong 35 × 20 cm (14 × 8 inches). Supporting the icing over the rolling pin, place it carefully over the 'shaft' and ring of the key. Dip your hands in cornflour and mould the icing over the cake to cover. Press the icing into the centre of the circle.

Trim the icing to fit all around the cake and knead the trimmings together. Roll out a strip to fit inside the edge of the circle. Place in position and smooth the joins with your fingers.

Cut the remaining icing in half and roll out each piece to an oblong large enough to cover the remaining pieces of the cake. Mould and trim to fit, then place them in position alongside the 'shaft' of the key, a little apart. Press against the cake to join.

Fit a greaseproof paper piping bag with a No. 7 star tube and fill with Royal icing. Pipe a row of shells around all top and bottom edges of the key, also down the sides of the smaller pieces of the key.

Colour 4 × 15 ml spoons (4 tablespoons) of icing pale pink with a few drops of pink food colouring. Fit a piping bag with a No. 2 plain piping tube and fill it with the pink icing. Pipe threads of icing underneath the shell edging around the top of the cake in an overlapping scallop design. Pipe reverse scallops over the top of the shell edging around the base of the key. Pipe beads of pink icing on each side of the shell edging around the top, sides and the base.

Outline the icing run-out numbers with beads of pink icing. Place the numbers on the top of the key cake and secure them with a little icing. If candles are required, make holders from the trimmings of icing and place them on the board.

Christening cake

Metric	Imperial
1 × 20 cm round Rich Fruit Cake (see pages 18–19)	*1 × 8 inch round Rich Fruit Cake (see pages 18–19)*
Apricot jam, boiled and sieved	*Apricot jam, boiled and sieved*
1 quantity Almond Paste (see page 32)	*1 quantity Almond Paste (see page 32)*
1 × 25 cm round silver cake board	*1 × 10 inch round silver cake board*
1 quantity Moulding Icing (see page 17))	*1 quantity Moulding Icing (see page 17)*

Decoration:
Pink food colouring
1 white plastic cocktail stick
10 cm 3-cm wide white lace
1 metre 3-cm wide shaded pink ribbon
1 quantity Royal Icing (see page 33)

Decoration:
Pink food colouring
1 white plastic cocktail stick
4 inches 1½-inch wide white lace
1 yard 1½-inch wide shaded pink ribbon
1 quantity Royal Icing (see page 33)

Cover the top and sides of the cake with apricot jam and then Almond paste. Place on the silver cake board. Cover the cake with moulding icing. Knead the trimmings together, using cornflour on your hands and the board, and colour two-thirds pale pink with food colouring.

To make the cradle, use a whole egg to shape the icing. Sprinkle the egg shell with cornflour and place the egg in an egg cup, rounded end upwards. Take a small piece of white icing and press it out with your fingers to an oval large enough just to curve over the egg. Mould lightly over the egg and trim the edge neatly with a knife. Leave to set.

Roll the trimmings into a thin pencil shape 5 cm (2 inches) long. Cut in half and place on the cradle for 'rockers'. Model a head and body for the baby. Take a small portion of pink icing and make a pillow and a cover. Mark a pattern on the cover with a knife. Roll out a long pencil shape of pink icing to fit around the cradle as a frill. Press flat with your fingers.

Remove the cradle from the egg and brush the top edge with a little water or egg white. Gently press the frill in position around the cradle. Trim and join at the top end of the cradle. Place the pillow, baby and cover in the cradle and put half a cocktail stick at the back of the pillow. Fold the lace in half, sew or staple the back edges together and place over the cocktail stick as a canopy.

Cut the ribbon to fit around the side of the cake and secure with a little icing. Make rosebuds from the remaining icing (see page 35).

Half fill a greaseproof paper piping bag fitted with a small star tube with Royal icing. Pipe a row of stars around the base of the cake on the cake board. On the top edge of the cake, pipe a row of stars a little apart, and on the side of the cake pipe a row of stars to alternate with the top row of stars. Mark an 8 cm (3½ inch) circle in the centre of the cake with a cutter and pipe small stars around the circle. Secure pink rosebuds to the circle of stars.

Colour the remaining Royal icing pale pink with a few drops of food colouring and, using a small plain piping tube, pipe threads of icing diagonally from the top to the bottom row of stars, at the top edge of the cake. Repeat in the opposite direction. Pipe a small bead of pink icing on top of each star on top of the cake and on the stars on the cake board. Place the cradle in the centre of the rosebuds on top of the cake.

To make the cradle

1. Press icing out to an oval for cradle. Make 2 'rockers'

2. Coat rounded end of an egg with cornflour and mould icing over; trim to size. Stick 'rockers' in position

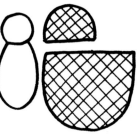

3. Make pillow and cover in pink icing. Mark quilting effect with back of a knife. Make baby in white icing

4. Roll out a narrow strip of pink icing to fit around cradle for frill

5. Fit frill to outside of cradle

6. Place pillow in cradle; put baby and cover on top. Place cocktail stick behind pillow and drape lace canopy over cocktail stick

SEASONAL CAKES

Christmas provides us with an occasion to make and decorate a special cake, but there are many other festivals to celebrate during the year. Each has its own theme and gives us opportunities for designing beautiful cakes.

Snow scene Christmas cake

Metric

1 × 20 cm round Rich Fruit Cake (see pages 18–19)
Apricot jam, boiled and sieved
1 quantity Almond Paste (see page 32)
1 × 25 cm round silver cake board
Royal Icing, made with 750 g icing sugar (see page 33)

Decorations
(see pages 28–29):
1 moulded Father Christmas with sack of presents
3 moulded Christmas trees

Imperial

1 × 8 inch round Rich Fruit Cake (see pages 18–19)
Apricot jam, boiled and sieved
1 quantity Almond Paste (see page 32)
1 × 10 inch round silver cake board
Royal Icing, made with 1½ lb icing sugar (see page 33)

Decorations
(see pages 28–29):
1 moulded Father Christmas with sack of presents
3 moulded Christmas trees

Cover the top and sides of the cake with apricot jam and then Almond paste. Place it on the cake board. Cover the cake completely with Royal icing until evenly coated. Press the tip of a small palette knife onto the surface of the icing and draw away to form a peak. Repeat to make peaks all over the cake. Leave a small area in the centre of the cake smooth.
Place the Father Christmas, sack of presents and trees in the centre of the cake on the smooth icing.

Christmas rose cake

Metric

1 × 17.5 cm square Rich Fruit Cake (see pages 18–19)
Apricot jam, boiled and sieved
1 quantity Almond Paste (see page 32)
1 × 22.5 cm square silver cake board
1 quantity Gelatine Icing (see page 17)

Decoration:
1 metre Christmas design ribbon
2 × 15 ml spoons Royal Icing (see page 33)

Imperial

1 × 7 inch square Rich Fruit Cake (see pages 18–19)
Apricot jam, boiled and sieved
1 quantity Almond Paste (see page 32)
1 × 9 inch square silver cake board
1 quantity Gelatine Icing (see page 17)

Decoration:
1 yard Christmas design ribbon
2 tablespoons Royal Icing (see page 33)

Cover the top and sides of the cake with apricot jam and then Almond paste. Place the cake on the silver cake board. Sprinkle a work surface with cornflour. Roll out the Gelatine icing to a 28 cm (11 in) square. Lift the icing on the rolling pin and place over the cake. Press the icing gently on to the top and side of the cake, working the icing down to the cake board and surplus icing to each corner. Snip off surplus icing from corners with scissors and trim the base of the cake with a sharp knife. Smooth the corners with fingers coated with cornflour.
Knead the icing trimmings together and use to make Christmas roses, ivy leaves, holly leaves and berries (see pages 28–29).
Measure the ribbon to fit around the cake and secure with a stainless steel pin or icing.
Put the Royal icing in a greaseproof paper piping bag fitted with a small star tube. Pipe a row of stars around the base of the cake on the cake board. On each corner of the cake, arrange two holly leaves, three berries and a Christmas rose. Place the remaining Christmas rose and a circle of ivy leaves in the centre of the cake. Secure all decorations with Royal icing.

Christmas rose cake; Snow scene Christmas cake; Lantern Christmas cake

Lantern Christmas cake

Metric

1 × 20 cm round Rich
Fruit Cake (see pages
18–19)
Apricot jam, boiled and
sieved
½ quantity Almond Paste
(see page 32)
1 × 25 cm round silver
cake board
1 cake frill

Imperial

1 × 8 inch round Rich
Fruit Cake (see pages
18–19)
Apricot jam, boiled and
sieved
½ quantity Almond Paste
(see page 32)
1 × 10 inch round silver
cake board
1 cake frill

Cover the top of the cake with apricot jam and then
Almond paste. Place the cake on the silver cake board. Use
the Almond paste trimmings to make a lantern, holly leaves
and berries, and mistletoe and berries (see pages 28–29).
Arrange alternate pairs of holly leaves and berries and
mistletoe leaves and berries around the top edge of the cake
and secure with a little jam. Place the lantern in the centre
of the cake on a small piece of Almond paste to raise it
slightly. Put the cake frill around the cake and secure with a
stainless steel pin.

Christmas scene cake

Metric	Imperial
1 × 20 cm square Rich Fruit Cake (see pages 18–19)	*1 × 8 inch square Rich Fruit Cake (see pages 18–19)*
Apricot jam, boiled and sieved	*Apricot jam, boiled and sieved*
1 quantity (1 kg) Almond Paste (see page 32)	*1 quantity (2 lb) Almond Paste (see page 32)*
1 × 25 cm square gold cake board	*1 × 10 inch square gold cake board*
Double quantity Royal Icing (see page 33)	*Double quantity Royal Icing (see page 33)*
Red, brown, green, yellow and black food colourings	*Red, brown, green, yellow and black food colourings*

Cover the cake with apricot jam and then Almond paste. Reserve the trimmings. Place the cake on the cake board. When the Almond paste is dry, cover the cake with three thin layers of Royal icing allowing the icing to dry between each coat. Keep the cake board clean during icing.

Fit a greaseproof paper piping bag with a No. 8 star tube and fill with Royal icing. Pipe a row of shells around the top and bottom edges of the cake.

Use the remaining icing to make a robin, Santa and a sleigh and reindeer run-outs; and the Almond paste trimmings to make holly and ivy leaves and berries (see pages 29, 31, and 36–37). When the run-outs are dry, peel off the paper. Using a little Royal icing, secure a Santa in sleigh with a reindeer to each side of the cake. Place the robin in the centre of the cake and arrange the holly and ivy leaves and berries underneath. Secure them with a little icing. Pipe a line of icing from the sleigh to the reindeer to join the two together. Pipe the whip from Santa's hands. Over-pipe with black or brown icing.

Miniature Christmas cakes

Metric	Imperial
1 × 20 cm round quantity Rich Fruit Cake mixture (see pages 18–19)	*1 × 8 inch round quantity Rich Fruit Cake mixture (see pages 18–19)*
Apricot jam, boiled and sieved	*Apricot jam, boiled and sieved*
1 quantity Almond Paste (see page 32)	*1 quantity Almond Paste (see page 32)*
4 × 18 cm round silver cake cards	*4 × 7 inch round silver cake cards*
¼ quantity Moulding Icing (see page 17)	*¼ quantity Moulding Icing (see page 17)*
1 quantity Royal Icing (see page 33)	*1 quantity Royal Icing (see page 33)*
Red, yellow and green food colourings	*Red, yellow and green food colourings*
3 paper holly sprigs with berries	*3 paper holly sprigs with berries*
1 Bambi decoration	*1 Bambi decoration*
1 metre 2.5-cm wide red Christmas ribbon	*1 yard 1-inch wide red Christmas ribbon*

Cooking time: 1¾–2 hours
Oven: 140°C, 275°F, Gas Mark 1

To make individual cake cases, cut out four 25 cm (10 inch) circles of double thickness foil and mould each around the base and side of an 850 g (1 lb 14 oz) can to make a 10 cm (4 inch) case. Remove from the can carefully and place the cake cases on a baking sheet covered with a double thickness of brown paper.

Divide the fruit cake mixture evenly between the foil cases and level the tops with the back of a spoon. (Weigh them to check that they are equally filled.) Bake in the centre of a preheated cool oven for 1¾ to 2 hours. Cool.

Remove the foil and cover each cake with apricot jam and then Almond paste, using 250 g (8 oz) for each cake. Place each cake on a silver card.

Cover two of the cakes with Moulding icing. Reserve the trimmings for the decorations. Smooth-ice the top of one cake with Royal icing. Cover the side of the cake and form peaks of icing using a small palette knife. Cover the remaining cake with Royal icing and form peaks all over.

Fit a greaseproof paper piping bag with a No. 6 star tube and fill with Royal icing. Pipe a row of shells around the top and bottom edge of one of the moulded cakes.

Using a No. 2 plain tube, pipe 'Merry Christmas' across the top of the smooth-iced cake. Colour 1 rounded 5 ml spoon (1 rounded teaspoon) of the icing red with food colouring. Using a No. 2 plain tube, pipe over the writing in red. Also pipe beads of red icing in between the shell edging around the top and bottom edges of the cake.

Make an icing run-out Christmas bell, and a Christmas rose, eight holly leaves and eight berries from the Moulding icing trimmings (see pages 28–29).

Arrange three holly leaves and berries on the 'Merry Christmas' cake. Place the Christmas rose in the centre of the plain moulded iced cake with five holly leaves radiating from the rose with a berry on each leaf. Wrap the ribbon around the cake. Put the Christmas bell in the centre of the piped cake and secure ribbon around the side. Put the Bambi figure and paper holly sprigs on the rough iced cake.

Christmas scene cake; Miniature Christmas cakes

Glacé fruit cake

Metric	Imperial
50 g blanched almonds	2 oz blanched almonds
125 g red, green and yellow glacé cherries	4 oz red, green and yellow glacé cherries
Candied angelica	Candied angelica
225 g butter	8 oz butter
225 g caster sugar	8 oz caster sugar
4 eggs, beaten	4 eggs, beaten
125 g ground almonds	4 oz ground almonds
Few drops of almond essence	Few drops of almond essence
50 g glacé pineapple, sliced	2 oz glacé pineapple, sliced
50 g crystallized ginger, sliced	2 oz crystallized ginger, sliced
225 g plain flour	8 oz plain flour
1 × 5 ml spoon baking powder	1 teaspoon baking powder
Apricot jam, boiled and sieved	Apricot jam, boiled and sieved
60 cm 5-cm wide green satin ribbon	2 feet 2-inch wide green satin ribbon
1 metre gold ribbon	1 yard gold ribbon

Cooking time: About 3½ hours
Oven: 140°C, 275°F, Gas Mark 1

Line the base and side of a 20 cm (8 inch) round cake tin with greaseproof paper. Tie a collar of brown paper or newspaper around the tin.

Split nine of the almonds in halves and reserve for decoration; cut the remainder into quarters. Rinse the syrup off the cherries and cut them in halves. On a large plate, arrange a design of cherries and almonds. Make a ring in the centre with six red cherry halves and place a yellow cherry half in the centre. Cut six large diamonds of angelica and arrange in between each red cherry, radiating out towards the edge of the plate. Arrange six red and six yellow cherry halves alternately around the edge, the yellow cherries towards the centre of the plate. Place a halved almond between each and one between the edge of the cake and each yellow cherry. Reserve the remaining cherries for the cake.

Cream the butter and sugar together until light and fluffy. Beat in the eggs a little at a time. Stir in the ground almonds and almond essence. Fold in the reserved almonds and cherries, then the glacé pineapple and the ginger.

Sift the flour and baking powder together and fold into the almond mixture with a metal spoon. Spread out in the tin, pressing down well, and level the surface with the back of the spoon. Transfer the cherries and almonds from the plate to make an identical design on top of the cake.

Bake in the centre of a preheated cool oven for about 3½ hours. Check after 2 hours and cover the cake with a piece of brown paper if the cake is sufficiently brown.

Leave in the tin until cold, then turn out. Remove the paper and store in a cake tin.

To serve, brush the top of the cake with apricot jam. Wrap the green ribbon around the cake and secure with a stainless steel pin. Tie the gold ribbon on top. Alternatively, use a cake frill.

Christmas ring cake

Metric	Imperial
½ quantity Glacé Fruit Cake mixture (see above)	½ quantity Glacé Fruit Cake mixture (see above)
Glacé Icing, made with 250 g icing sugar (see page 13)	Glacé Icing, made with 8 oz icing sugar (see page 13)
3 glacé pineapple rings	3 glacé pineapple rings
Glacé peaches and pears	Glacé peaches and pears
6 glacé cherries	6 glacé cherries
Candied angelica	Candied angelica

Cooking time: 2½–2¾ hours
Oven: 140°C, 275°F, Gas Mark 1

Grease a 500 ml (18 fl oz) capacity ring mould. Spread the cake mixture in the mould. Bake in a preheated cool oven for 2½ to 2¾ hours. Invert the cake onto a cooling rack and leave to cool.

To decorate, place the cake on a serving plate and coat the top with Glacé icing, allowing the icing to run down the side. When the icing is partially set, arrange the glacé fruits on the top at one side and in the centre. Cut the angelica into diamonds and arrange on the top and between the glacé fruits.

Glacé fruit cake; Christmas ring cake

Father Christmas cake

Metric	Imperial
1 quantity Moulding Icing (see page 17)	*1 quantity Moulding Icing (see page 17)*
Red and brown or black food colourings	*Red and brown or black food colourings*
175 g quantity Quick Mix Cake mixture, baked in 900 and 300 ml pudding basins (see pages 20–21)	*6 oz quantity Quick Mix Cake mixture, baked in 1½ and ½ pint pudding basins (see pages 20–21)*
1 × 20 cm round silver cake board	*1 × 8 inch round silver cake board*
Apricot jam, boiled and sieved	*Apricot jam, boiled and sieved*

The cake mixture in the 300 ml (½ pint) pudding basin should be cooked for 50 to 55 minutes.

Colour two-thirds of the icing bright red with red food colouring. Put the icing in a polythene bag to prevent drying.

Cut the remaining piece of icing in half and colour one piece flesh colour with red and brown colourings. Colour a very small piece of the remaining icing black or brown. Put the white icing in a polythene bag to prevent drying.

Put the larger cake on the cake board for the 'body' and brush with apricot jam. Sprinkle a work surface with cornflour. Roll out one-third of the red icing to a rectangle 25 × 10 cm (10 × 4 inches). Wrap around the front half and top of the body and trim to fit.

Roll out the black or brown icing to a strip 20 × 1 cm (8 × ½ inch) for a belt and stick around the body. Cut out a small white square buckle and place on the centre of the belt.

Brush the flat base and side of the small cake with jam.

Roll out the flesh-coloured icing 5 cm (2 inches) larger than the base of the cake. Put the icing over the base of the cake and mould the surplus around the side of the cake. Put the small cake on top of the body, with the flat side facing front for the head.

Roll out another one-third of the red icing to a rectangle 25 × 10 cm (10 × 4 inches). Cut the sides at an angle to form a cloak shape. Place the icing cloak around the back of the body, allowing the icing to fall into folds. Press the cloak in around the neck and allow it to hang away from the body at the front edges.

Roll the remaining red icing into a rectangle 30 × 10 cm (12 × 4 inches) and wrap around the head for a hood. Allow the hood to hang away from the side of the face. Trim the back of the hood and press into the neck. Form the surplus icing into a point at the back of the head like a hood and smooth the join with a palette knife.

Clean the work top to remove all traces of red icing, then roll out pencil-sized lengths of white icing. Use these to trim the edges of the cloak, hood and around the neck. Make a large white ball for a bobble and secure on top of the hood. With the remaining white icing make a beard shape, moustache and hair. Make two white eyebrows and a red nose. Make two flesh coloured eyes and mark pupils with colouring. Place all features in position on the face.

Yule log

Metric	Imperial
1 unfilled chocolate-flavoured Swiss Roll (see page 22)	*1 unfilled chocolate-flavoured Swiss Roll (see page 22)*
1 quantity Chocolate Fudge Frosting (see pages 14–15)	*1 quantity Chocolate Fudge Frosting (see pages 14–15)*
1 × 18 cm round silver cake board	*1 × 7 inch round silver cake board*
50 g icing sugar, sifted	*2 oz icing sugar, sifted*
1 × 5 ml spoon boiling water	*1 teaspoon boiling water*
Robin and sprigs of holly	*Robin and sprigs of holly*

Unroll the Swiss roll and spread with some of the chocolate frosting. Roll up and cut a 5 cm (2 inch) piece off one end of the roll at an angle. Arrange both pieces on the cake board with the small piece at the side of the large piece of Swiss roll to represent a branch.

Cover the cake with the remaining chocolate frosting and mark it with a palette knife to give a tree bark effect. Sift a little of the icing sugar over the log to represent snow.

Put the remaining sugar in a bowl. Add enough water to mix to a stiff piping consistency. Put the icing in a greaseproof paper icing bag. Fold down the top and snip the point from the end. Pipe rings of icing at all ends of the log to represent the grain of the wood. Arrange a robin and sprigs of holly on top. Sprinkle the board with more icing sugar.

Father Christmas cake; Yule log

Valentine sweetheart cake

Metric	Imperial
200 g quantity lemon-flavoured Quick Mix Cake mixture (see pages 20–21)	*8 oz quantity lemon-flavoured Quick Mix Cake mixture (see pages 20–21)*
Lemon curd	*Lemon curd*
Apricot jam, boiled and sieved	*Apricot jam, boiled and sieved*
1 × 20 cm round silver cake board	*1 × 8 inch round silver cake board*
1 quantity Satin Icing (see page 17)	*1 quantity Satin Icing (see page 17)*
Pink food colouring	*Pink food colouring*
Royal Icing, made with 1 egg white and 175–225 g icing sugar (omit glycerine) (see page 33)	*Royal Icing, made with 1 egg white and 6–8 oz icing sugar (omit glycerine) (see page 33)*
Shaded pink sugar-frosted flowers (see page 26)	*Shaded pink sugar-frosted flowers (see page 26)*

If using a round cake tin, cut and shape into a heart as shown

Cooking time: 1 hour 10–15 minutes
Oven: 160°C, 325°F, Gas Mark 3

Grease and line a 20 cm (8 inch) heart-shaped cake tin. Spread the cake mixture in the tin and bake in a preheated moderate oven for 1 hour and 10 to 15 minutes.

Allow to cool, then remove from the tin and cut into two layers. Sandwich with lemon curd.

If a heart-shaped tin is not available, use a deep 20 cm (8 inch) round tin. After baking, cut the cake to a heart-shape by cutting out a 'V' shape, 3.5 cm (1½ inches) deep and 16 cm (6½ inches) wide at the top. Cut the piece in half and place the halves on the opposite sides of the cake, reversing positions to form a point, trimming on the centre line. Stick together with jam and trim the cake to a good shape (see diagram).

Place the cake on the cake board and brush the cake all over with apricot jam. Colour the Satin icing pale pink with a few drops of food colouring. Sprinkle a work surface with cornflour and roll out the icing to a circle 5 cm (2 inches) larger than the top of the cake. Lift the icing on the rolling pin and lay over the cake. Dip your hands in cornflour and smooth the icing over the top and down the sides of the cake. Trim the surplus icing from the base of the cake with a knife.

Fill a greaseproof paper piping bag fitted with a No. 8 star tube with the Royal icing. Pipe a row of scrolls around the top and bottom edge of the cake. Arrange sugar-frosted flowers on top of the cake and place a few at the side of the cake on the cake board.

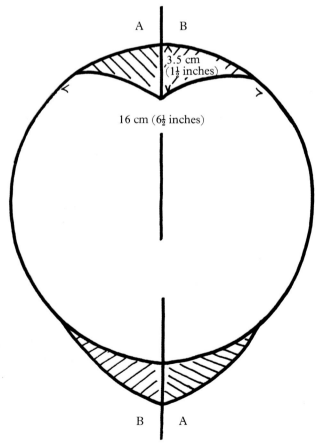

A B
3.5 cm (1½ inches)
16 cm (6½ inches)
B A

Mother's Day flower basket cake

Metric

1 chocolate-flavoured Torten Sponge Cake (see page 23)
Double quantity chocolate-flavoured Butter Icing (see page 13)
1 × 20 cm round silver cake board
½ quantity Moulding Icing (see page 17)
Green, brown, purple and yellow food colourings

Imperial

1 chocolate-flavoured Torten Sponge Cake (see page 23)
Double quantity chocolate-flavoured Butter Icing (see page 13)
1 × 8 inch round silver cake board
½ quantity Moulding Icing (see page 17)
Green, brown, purple and yellow food colourings

Cut the cake into three layers. Sandwich the layers together with some of the Butter icing. Place the torten on the cake board and spread the top and sides with a thin layer of icing. Fit a greaseproof paper piping bag with a ribbon tube and fill with the remaining icing. Pipe a basketwork design onto the side and half of the top of the cake (see diagrams).

Colour a small piece of the moulding icing dark green with food colouring. Cut the remaining icing into three portions. Colour the icing brown, purple and yellow with food colourings.

Sprinkle a board with cornflour and roll out the brown icing to a semi-circle to fit half of the top of the cake. Mark a lattice design over the surface using the back of a knife. Leave this basket lid to set.

Make violets from the purple icing and forsythia from the yellow icing. Mould the leaf shapes from the green icing.

When the flowers, leaves and basket lid are set, put the lid carefully in position and secure with a little icing. Place a few forsythia flowers on the cake at each side under the lid. Arrange the remaining leaves and flowers under the lid and secure with icing.

To pipe the basketwork design

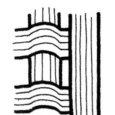

2. Pipe a second vertical line on top of the horizontal lines about 2.5 mm (⅛ inch) apart

1. Using a ribbon piping tube, pipe one vertical line from the top to the bottom on the side of the cake. Pipe horizontal lines 5 mm (¼ inch) apart across the vertical line

3. Pipe horizontal lines between the first row of horizontal lines to make a basket design. Repeat from the beginning

63

SEASONAL CAKES
Simnel cake

Metric	Imperial
½ quantity Almond Paste (see page 32)	½ quantity Almond Paste (see page 32)
200 g sultanas	8 oz sultanas
100 g currants	4 oz currants
100 g raisins	4 oz raisins
50 g mixed cut peel	2 oz mixed cut peel
50 g glacé cherries, halved	2 oz glacé cherries, halved
Grated rind and juice of 1 small orange	Grated rind and juice of 1 small orange
100 g self-raising flour	4 oz self-raising flour
100 g plain flour	4 oz plain flour
1 × 5 ml spoon ground cinnamon	1 teaspoon ground cinnamon
3 eggs	3 eggs
150 g butter, softened	6 oz butter, softened
150 g moist brown sugar	6 oz moist brown sugar

Decoration:	Decoration:
1 egg, separated	1 egg, separated
1 × 5 ml spoon water	1 teaspoon water
150 g icing sugar	6 oz icing sugar
1 × 5 ml spoon glycerine	1 teaspoon glycerine
Easter chick	Easter chick
Small chocolate Easter eggs	Small chocolate Easter eggs
1 metre 7.5-cm wide gold lace ribbon	1 yard 2½-inch wide gold lace ribbon

Cooking time: About 3 hours
Oven: 160°C, 325°F, Gas Mark 3

Line the base and side of an 18 cm (7 inch) round cake tin. Measure round the tin with a piece of string and cut to the exact size. Reserve the string.

Roll out half of the Almond paste to a circle the size of the cake tin.

Mix together the sultanas, currants, raisins, mixed peel, cherries and orange rind and juice in a large bowl. Turn the fruit to coat in orange juice. Sift the flours and cinnamon into another bowl. Add the eggs, butter and sugar and mix until well blended. Beat for 1 to 2 minutes or until the mixture is smooth and glossy. Add the fruit mixture and mix well.

Spread half of the cake mixture into the prepared tin and level the surface with the back of a spoon. Put the circle of almond paste on top, then cover with the remaining cake mixture.

Bake in a preheated moderate oven for about 3 hours, or until the cake begins to shrink from the side of the tin. It should spring back when pressed with the fingers.

Meanwhile, cut the remaining Almond paste into three. Roll each piece between your hands to form a long roll, the length of the measured piece of string. Plait the rolls together.

Beat the egg yolk with the water. Arrange the plait of Almond paste around the edge of the cake and brush the top and sides with the egg yolk mixture. Cover the centre of the cake with a circle of foil, if it is sufficiently brown. Return the cake to the oven to bake for 10 minutes or until the Almond paste plait is browned.

Leave the cake to cool in the tin.

To decorate, make Royal icing with the egg white, icing sugar and glycerine (see page 33). Pour into the centre of the cake and leave to set.

Place an Easter chicken and some chocolate eggs on the icing.

Cut the ribbon to fit the cake. (If using satin ribbon, cut a strip of greaseproof paper to fit around the cake. Stick onto the ribbon.) Secure to the cake with stainless steel pins.

Nest cakes

Metric	Imperial
1 quantity chocolate-flavoured Butter Icing (see page 13)	1 quantity chocolate-flavoured Butter Icing (see page 13)
100 g quantity Quick Mix Cake mixture, baked in 18 paper cake cases (see pages 20–21)	4 oz quantity Quick Mix Cake mixture, baked in 18 paper cake cases (see pages 20–21)
36 small sugar-coated Easter eggs	36 small sugar-coated Easter eggs

Pipe a swirl of icing with a star tube on each cake, starting from the outside edge and finishing in the centre.
Decorate each with two small sugar Easter eggs.
Makes 18 cakes

Simnel cake; Nest cakes

Halloween cake

Metric	Imperial
100 g quantity chocolate-flavoured Quick Mix Cake mixture, baked in 2 × 1.2 l basins (see pages 20–21)	*4 oz quantity chocolate-flavoured Quick Mix Cake mixture, baked in 2 × 2 pint basins (see pages 20–21)*
½ quantity Butter Icing (see page 13)	*½ quantity Butter Icing (see page 13)*
1 × 18 cm round silver cake board	*1 × 7 inch round silver cake board*
1 quantity Moulding or Satin Icing (see page 17)	*1 quantity Moulding or Satin Icing (see page 17)*
Yellow, red, green and black food colourings	*Yellow, red, green and black food colourings*
12 cloves	*12 cloves*
1 cocktail stick	*1 cocktail stick*

Cut each cake into two layers, then sandwich together with Butter icing. Sandwich the flat side of each cake together with Butter icing to make a ball shape. Place the cake on the cake board. Cut a shallow circle from the centre of the top of the cake. Mark the cake in eight sections from the centre of the top and down the side. With a small knife cut a small ridge from the cake down each marked line.

Cut off one-third of the Moulding or Satin icing and reserve in a polythene bag. Colour the remainder yellow and reserve a small piece in a polythene bag. Add a little red colouring to the larger piece of yellow icing to tint it a pale orange colour. Roll out on a board lightly dusted with cornflour to a 20 cm (8 inch) circle. Lift on the rolling pin and lay over the centre of the cake. Dip your fingers in cornflour and smooth the icing over the cake, pressing gently into the grooves. Trim off the surplus icing and reserve.

Mix red and yellow colouring on a plate to make orange; lightly paint the grooves with the colouring. Shape some of the reserved yellow icing to represent the hollowed out eyes, nose and mouth for the Jack o'lantern and press into position.

Colour a small piece of the white icing green. Mould four leaves and a stalk and place in position in the centre of the cake. Make six apples as directed on pages 24–25 and paint with red colouring. Place a clove in each for the stalk and place on the board.

Reserve a walnut-sized piece of white icing, then colour one-quarter of the remaining icing bright orange and the remainder black (mix blue colouring with brown or gravy caramel, if black is not available).

Mould six oranges with the bright orange icing and place a clove in each. Place on the board. Make a witch's broomstick handle with more bright orange icing and roll tiny strands of the pale orange icing for the bristles of the broom. Press onto the broomstick handle and place on the silver board.

Mould bats, a witches' cauldron and witches' hats from black icing. Mould coals from bright orange icing. Paint red and place on the board. Place the witches' cauldron on top when set.

To make the witch, first press a cocktail stick into a potato to hold it steady while moulding. Form a sausage-shaped piece of white icing 3.5 cm (1½ inches) long for the body and press onto the cocktail stick. Press a round head made from pale orange icing on top.

Shape a hooked nose and roll a piece of bright orange icing for the mouth and two tiny balls of black icing for the eyes. Press into position (stick with egg white, if necessary). Roll fine strands of yellow icing for the hair and place a witch's hat on top. Dip your fingers in cornflour and press out a 5 × 7.5 cm (2 × 3 inch) triangle of black icing for the cloak. Press the corners round. Drape around the body and turn the neck edge back for the collar.

Remove the cocktail stick carefully from the potato. Press the cocktail stick with the witch into the top of the cake. Make a black cat with an arched back as shown on pages 24–25. Place beside the witch.

Harvest festival cake

Metric

1 × 20 cm round Rich Fruit Cake (see pages 18–19)
Apricot jam, boiled and sieved
1 quantity Almond Paste (see page 32)
1 × 25 cm round silver cake board
1½ quantity Gelatine or Moulding Icing (see page 17)

Decoration:
Red, brown, yellow, orange, green, blue and purple food colourings
Glacé Icing (see page 13)
1 metre 2.5-cm wide embroidered brown ribbon

Imperial

1 × 8 inch round Rich Fruit Cake (see pages 18–19)
Apricot jam, boiled and sieved
1 quantity Almond Paste (see page 32)
1 × 10 inch round silver cake board
1½ quantity Gelatine or Moulding Icing (see page 17)

Decoration:
Red, brown, yellow, orange, green, blue and purple food colourings
Glacé Icing (see page 13)
1¼ yards 1¼-inch wide embroidered brown ribbon

Cover the top and side of the cake with apricot jam and then Almond paste. Place on the cake board. Cover the cake with two thirds of the Gelatine or Moulding icing.

To make the decorations, cut the remaining icing into five pieces. Colour one piece red, one corn by mixing brown and yellow, one orange, one green and leave one white. Make moulded fruits as instructed on pages 24–25: make plums and cherries, then add blue to the remaining red icing to make purple for the grapes. Make vegetables in a similar way. Paint white turnips and cabbages with purple colouring and other vegetables with brown or gravy caramel colouring. Arrange on the top edge of the cake and around the board, securing with a little Glacé icing. Place some in a trug made from corn-coloured icing, if desired. To make the harvest sheaf, shape a keyhole piece of corn-coloured icing, pressing out the shape with your fingers dipped in cornflour. Roll pieces for the stalks and stick to the base with egg white. Roll out a piece and cut it into strips, then into diamonds for the ears. Mark each with a knife, then attach in overlapping rows with egg white. Make a tie with some icing for the sheaf.

Mould a tiny white or brown mouse with a curly tail and stick to the sheaf with egg white. Place the sheaf in the centre of the cake and secure it with a little Glacé icing. Arrange ribbon around the cake and secure it with a stainless steel pin.

NOVELTY CAKES

Let the birthday child choose from the cakes in this chapter. They are as much fun to make as to receive.

Teddy bear cake

Metric	Imperial
1 quantity orange-flavoured Butter Icing (see page 13)	1 quantity orange-flavoured Butter Icing (see page 13)
Orange food colouring	Orange food colouring
1 × 20 cm round silver cake board	1 × 8 inch round silver cake board
1 jam-filled Swiss Roll (see page 22)	1 jam-filled Swiss Roll (see page 22)
5 bought filled mini Swiss Rolls	5 bought filled mini Swiss Rolls

Decoration:

25 g desiccated coconut	1 oz desiccated coconut
Green food colouring	Green food colouring
1 × 15 ml spoon apricot jam	1 tablespoon apricot jam
2 sultanas	2 sultanas
½ glacé cherry	½ glacé cherry
3 small jelly sweets	3 small jelly sweets
25 g currants	1 oz currants
½ metre 1-cm wide red ribbon	½ yard ½-inch wide red ribbon
Birthday candles	Birthday candles

Colour the Butter icing with a few drops of orange food colouring. Put the coconut and a few drops of green colouring in a small bowl and mix together until evenly coloured. Spread apricot jam on the cake board and cover with the green coconut.

Cut a 5 cm (2 inch) slice from the large Swiss roll. Spread the remaining piece of large Swiss roll with Butter icing and place upright at the back of the cake board. Place the small slice of Swiss roll on top to form a 'head'. Cover with icing, shaping it into a face by building up a nose and rounding the head.

Spread two mini Swiss rolls with icing and place on the board at angles to the body for legs. Cut a wedge-shaped piece from the ends of two of the remaining mini Swiss rolls and cover with Butter icing. Place these rolls at the top of the body, resting on the legs, for arms, with the wedge ends towards the body. Build up the shoulders with more icing.

Cut two 2.5 cm (1 inch) slices from the last mini Swiss roll for ears. Cover with icing and place in position on the head. Smooth the icing over the teddy and mark in features. Place two sultanas in position for the eyes, and the half glacé cherry for the nose. Put three jelly sweets down the front for buttons. Arrange currants in a semi-circle at the base of the arms and legs for 'pads'. Make a bow tie from the ribbon and press onto the icing to secure.

Press candles into sweets and place on the cake board, or coat the remaining piece of mini Swiss roll in icing to press in candles.

Ears:
2 slices mini Swiss rolls

Head:
5 cm (2 inch) slice of large Swiss roll

Body:
1 large Swiss roll (with slice cut off for head)

Arms:
2 mini Swiss rolls with wedges cut off one end

Legs:
2 mini Swiss rolls

Football match cake

Metric

175 g quantity of
chocolate-flavoured
Quick Mix Cake mixture,
baked in a 27.5 × 18 cm
oblong tin (see pages
20–21)
1 quantity vanilla-
flavoured Butter Icing
(see page 13)
25 g desiccated coconut
Green food colouring
4 × 15 ml spoons icing
sugar
1 × 150 g packet
chocolate finger biscuits
Footballer figures and
goal posts

Imperial

6 oz quantity of
chocolate-flavoured
Quick Mix Cake mixture,
baked in an 11 × 7 inch
oblong tin (see pages
20–21)
1 quantity vanilla-
flavoured Butter Icing
(see page 13)
1 oz desiccated coconut
Green food colouring
4 tablespoons icing sugar
1 × 5 oz packet chocolate
finger biscuits
Footballer figures and
goal posts

Cover an oblong 30 × 20 cm (12 × 8 inch) board with foil.
Cut the cake into two layers, then sandwich together with
one-third of the Butter icing. Place, base upwards, on the
board. Spread the top and sides with Butter icing,
reserving a small amount. Mix the remaining Butter icing
with a little coconut and form into a football.

Mix the remaining coconut in a bowl with a few drops of
green colouring until evenly coloured. Sprinkle over the
top of the cake to represent grass. Draw the point of a knife
through the coconut 1.25 cm ($\frac{1}{2}$ inch) from the edges for the
boundary lines of the football pitch. Mark the other lines.
Mix the icing sugar with a little hot water and place in a
piping bag without a tube. Snip off the end and pipe icing
along the lines.

Cut each chocolate finger biscuit in half and place, cut ends
downwards, around the cake.

Arrange goal posts in position and put the football figures
and the football on the field.

Summer holiday cake

Metric

Golden syrup
1 × 20 cm square silver cake board
100 g quantity Quick Mix Cake mixture baked in an 18 cm square cake tin (see pages 20–21)
½ quantity chocolate-flavoured Butter Icing (see page 13)
25 g desiccated coconut
Green and blue food colouring
Demerara sugar
Liquorice allsorts
Dolly mixture sweets
Chocolate matchstick sweets
Rice paper
2 drinking straws
Cocktail sticks
2 × 15 ml spoons icing sugar

Imperial

Golden syrup
1 × 10 inch square silver cake board
4 oz quantity Quick Mix Cake mixture, baked in a 7 inch square cake tin (see pages 20–21)
½ quantity chocolate-flavoured Butter Icing (see page 13)
1 oz desiccated coconut
Green and blue food colouring
Demerara sugar
Liquorice allsorts
Dolly mixture sweets
Chocolate matchstick sweets
Rice paper
2 drinking straws
Cocktail sticks
2 tablespoons icing sugar

Spread golden syrup in a 2.5 cm (1 inch) band around the edge of the cake board. Put the cake in the centre of the board. Cut the cake at one side to form 'coves'; reserve the cake pieces. Spread the exposed board with golden syrup. Cover the top and the sides of the cake with Butter icing. Cover the reserved pieces of cake with Butter icing and arrange in one corner of the cake to represent boulders.

Reserve a little coconut and put the remainder in a bowl. Add a few drops of green food colouring and mix until evenly coloured. Sprinkle green coconut over the top of the cake to represent grass; place a little on the 'boulders' at the back and the 'cliffs' at the front.

Add blue colouring to the remaining green coconut. Sprinkle around the edges of the board to represent the sea; sprinkle some on the grass to represent a stream.

Sprinkle the board in the 'cove' with demerara sugar to represent sand. Sprinkle white coconut where it joins the 'sea' to represent surf. Make a 'seat', 'table', 'trees' and a 'fence' with liquorice allsorts and dolly mixture sweets. Make a fence and steps down to the 'sea' with halved chocolate matchstick sweets. Make a seat and a fire from more matchstick sweets. Use a round red sweet for the fire coals. Make steps down to the beach with coloured chocolate beans.

To make the tent, cut two pieces of rice paper each 6 × 4 cm (2½ × 1½ inches) and four triangular pieces for the ends. Form into a tent shape, using pieces of drinking straw for the 'tent poles' and halved cocktail sticks for the 'tent pegs'.

Cut liquorice sandwich sweets to make boat shapes and spear with sails made from squares of paper and cocktail sticks.

Mix the icing sugar with a drop of water. Place in a paper piping bag without a tube and snip off the end. Pipe a 'waterfall' from the rocks down to the stream.

Make a flag by sticking a piece of paper onto a drinking straw and press into the cake. Write the name of the birthday child on the flag.

Gingerbread house

Metric	Imperial
400 g plain flour	*1 lb plain flour*
2 × 15 ml spoons ground mixed spice	*2 tablespoons ground mixed spice*
8 × 15 ml spoons golden syrup	*8 tablespoons golden syrup*
75 g margarine	*3 oz margarine*
75 g soft dark brown sugar	*3 oz soft dark brown sugar*
1 × 15 ml spoon bicarbonate of soda	*1 tablespoon bicarbonate of soda*
2 × 15 ml spoons water	*2 tablespoons water*
1 egg	*1 egg*
1 egg yolk	*1 egg yolk*
1 quantity Quick American Frosting (see page 15)	*1 quantity Quick American Frosting (see page 15)*
1 × 25 cm square silver cake board	*1 × 10 inch square silver cake board*

Decoration:
Assorted sweets
Moulded dog
(see pages 24–25)

Decoration:
Assorted sweets
Moulded dog
(see pages 24–25)

Cooking time: 20–30 minutes
Oven: 190°C, 375°F, Gas Mark 5

Line two baking sheets with non-stick baking parchment. Following the diagrams given here, cut out the card shapes for the roof, end and side walls of the house.

Sift the flour and spice into a bowl. Measure the golden syrup carefully, levelling off the spoon with a knife and making sure there is none on the underside of the spoon, and put in a saucepan with the margarine and sugar. Stir over a low heat until the sugar has dissolved.

Dissolve the bicarbonate of soda in the water in a bowl, then add to the dry ingredients with the syrup mixture, egg and egg yolk. Mix together with a wooden spoon to form a soft dough.

Cut off half of the dough and put in a polythene bag. Roll out the other half to a 6 mm (¼ inch) thickness. Cut out one of each shape: roof, end and side wall from the dough and arrange on a baking sheet. Bake on the second shelf from the top in a preheated moderately hot oven for 8 to 10 minutes or until risen and golden brown. Leave to cool on the baking sheet for a few minutes, then transfer to a wire rack to cool completely.

Knead the trimmings together with the dough from the polythene bag. Roll out the dough and cut out another roof, end and side wall. Bake as above.

Knead together all the trimmings and cut out two doors, two doorsteps, one path, four square windows, two rectangular windows and two chimney pieces (see diagrams). Bake for 5 to 8 minutes, then cool on a wire rack. Spread a little of the frosting on all edges of the sides and end walls. Put together on the cake board, towards the back, like a box and press the pieces lightly together. Fill the inside with sweets, if desired.

Spread frosting along the remaining top edges of the house where the roof is fixed. Also spread frosting underneath the roof about 2.5 cm (1 inch) in from the edge where the roof joins the walls and along the top edge of the roof.

Carefully place both roof pieces in position using more frosting along the top join if necessary. Hold in position for 3 to 4 minutes or place supports underneath the roof until it has set. Leave the cake at this stage for about 1 hour before decorating.

Put a door, doorstep and rectangular windows at the front and back of the house in position. Secure with a little frosting. Place two square windows on each side wall and secure with frosting. Put the path in front of the house on the cake board. Cover the roof, tops of windows and the doors with frosting. Pull points of icing down with a small knife to represent snow over the roof, windows and doors. Trim some gingerbread off the chimney. Sandwich the chimney pieces together with some frosting, place in position on the roof and secure with a cocktail stick, if necessary. Cover the top and side of the chimney with frosting. Arrange coloured sweets around the windows, doors and roof to decorate.

Spread the remaining frosting over the cake board and arrange some sweets around the edge of the board. Put the moulded dog on the path in front of the door. Make some flowers by sticking a round flat sweet onto a long thin sweet with frosting. Stick into the frosting on the board.

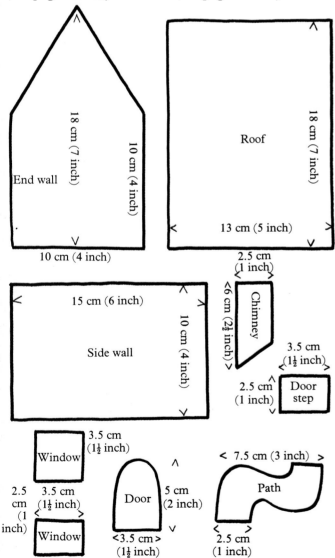

End wall — 18 cm (7 inch), 10 cm (4 inch), 10 cm (4 inch)

Roof — 18 cm (7 inch), 13 cm (5 inch)

Side wall — 15 cm (6 inch), 10 cm (4 inch)

Chimney — 2.5 cm (1 inch), 6 cm (2½ inch), 3.5 cm (1½ inch)

Door step — 2.5 cm (1 inch)

Window — 3.5 cm (1½ inch), 2.5 cm (1 inch)

Door — 5 cm (2 inch), 3.5 cm (1½ inch)

Path — 7.5 cm (3 inch), 2.5 cm (1 inch)

Kevin kitten

Metric

*175 g quantity Quick
Mix Cake mixture, baked
in 900 and 300 ml pudding
basins (see pages 20–21)
1 quantity chocolate-
flavoured Butter Icing
(see page 13)*

Decoration:
*100 g desiccated coconut
Green food colouring
1 × 15 ml spoon apricot
jam
1 × 18 cm round silver
cake board
50 g Almond Paste
(see page 32)
Blue food colouring
1 length spaghetti
3 blue cocktail sticks
3 red sweets
¼ metre 1-cm wide blue
ribbon
Birthday candles*

Imperial

*6 oz quantity Quick
Mix Cake mixture, baked
in 1½ and ½ pint pudding
basins (see pages 20–21)
1 quantity chocolate-
flavoured Butter Icing
(see page 13)*

Decoration:
*4 oz desiccated coconut
Green food colouring
1 tablespoon apricot
jam
1 × 7 inch round silver
cake board
2 oz Almond Paste
(see page 32)
Blue food colouring
1 length spaghetti
3 blue cocktail sticks
3 red sweets
¼ yard ½-inch wide blue
ribbon
Birthday candles*

The cake mixture in the 300 ml (½ pint) pudding basin should be cooked for 50 to 55 minutes.

Place 25 g (1 oz) of the coconut and a few drops of green food colouring in a small bowl. Mix together until evenly coloured. Spread apricot jam over the cake board and cover with the green coconut.

Coat both cakes with chocolate icing, then roll each in the remaining uncoloured coconut until evenly covered.

Put the larger cake on the cake board. Place the smaller cake on top with the flat side facing the back. Secure and build up with more icing, then cover the icing with coconut. Form two balls of Almond paste for eyes. Colour the remaining paste blue with a few drops of blue food colouring. Cut in half, then cut one half into two pieces and shape each piece into an ear. Use the remaining blue Almond paste to make a long tail, a nose, two 'pupils' for the eyes and a mouth.

Thread ears onto two pieces of spaghetti and secure in position on the head. Place the remaining features in position. Break each cocktail stick in half and place three at each side of the mouth for whiskers. Arrange the red sweets down the front of the body, and make a bow tie with blue ribbon. Secure around the neck with a little icing. Arrange birthday candles around the cake board.

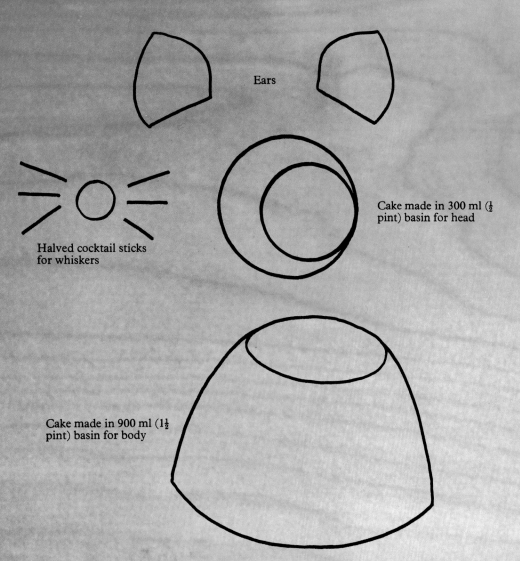

Ears

Halved cocktail sticks
for whiskers

Cake made in 300 ml (½
pint) basin for head

Cake made in 900 ml (1½
pint) basin for body

Puffing Billy steam train cake

Metric

1 × 20 cm square silver cake board
Apricot jam, boiled and sieved
2 × 15 ml spoons desiccated coconut, toasted
3 × 15 ml spoons desiccated coconut
Green food colouring
3 bought filled mini Swiss Rolls
1 chocolate-flavoured Swiss Roll (see page 22)
Orange-flavoured Butter Icing, made with 150 g icing sugar, 75 g butter and 1.5 × 5 ml spoons orange juice (see page 13)
1 × 5 ml spoon cocoa powder
1 × 5 ml spoon boiling water
4 liquorice bars
1 cocktail stick
2 digestive biscuits
6 biscuits from All Butter Shortcake Assortment
Liquorice allsorts
Dolly mixture sweets
Birthday candles
Small round lollipops
1 × 15 cm round silver cake board

Imperial

1 × 8 inch square silver cake board
Apricot jam, boiled and sieved
2 tablespoons desiccated coconut, toasted
3 tablespoons desiccated coconut
Green food colouring
3 bought filled mini Swiss Rolls
1 chocolate-flavoured Swiss Roll (see page 22)
Orange-flavoured Butter Icing, made with 6 oz icing sugar, 3 oz butter and 1½ teaspoons orange juice (see page 13)
1 teaspoon cocoa powder
1 teaspoon boiling water
4 liquorice bars
1 cocktail stick
2 digestive biscuits
6 biscuits from All Butter Shortcake Assortment
Liquorice allsorts
Dolly mixture sweets
Birthday candles
Small round lollipops
1 × 6 inch round silver cake board

Brush a 7.5 cm (3 inch) diagonal strip of jam across the square cake board and sprinkle with toasted coconut. Put the white coconut in a bowl. Add a few drops of green colouring and mix until evenly coloured. Brush the remainder of the board with jam and sprinkle with green coconut.

Cut a thin slice from the tops of two mini Swiss rolls, so they will lie flat, and place the rolls end to end in the toasted coconut section.

Cut a 2.5 cm (1 inch) slice from the end of the chocolate Swiss roll and a 2.5 cm (1 inch) slice from the top of the end; reserve the pieces.

Put 4 × 15 ml spoons (4 tablespoons) of the icing in a bowl. Dissolve the cocoa in the boiling water and add to the icing. Mix until evenly coloured. Set aside.

Cover the remaining mini Swiss roll with uncoloured icing and reserve. Colour the remaining icing pale green with food colouring. Spread over the large Swiss roll and place on the mini rolls on the cake board.

Cut the liquorice into strips and place two strips around the 'engine'. Place strips on the board for lines. Make two rings with liquorice on the orange mini Swiss roll for the funnel. Place a cocktail stick in the end of the engine and press the end of the funnel into it.

Spread one side of each digestive biscuit with some of the brown icing and arrange liquorice strips on them to represent the spokes of a wheel.

Press two round piped shortcake biscuits for front wheels and two for top wheels at the back onto the engine. Place the large wheels alongside and secure with icing. Put a large oblong biscuit on the cut out section at the back and a small one in front of the train. Cut one round pink sweet in half to make it thinner and attach one half to each front wheel with icing.

Cover the reserved round slice of large Swiss roll with the remaining brown icing. Place at the back of the train on the reserved wedge of Swiss roll. Arrange dolly mixture sweets on the roll and sweets around and on the engine. Place a black tube sweet on the funnel and attach some cotton wool smoke with icing. Arrange a ring of sweets on the front of the engine and a round dolly mixture sweet in the centre. Decorate the board with more sweets. Press candles into striped square sweets.

Arrange lollipops for signals and the remaining sweets on the round silver board.

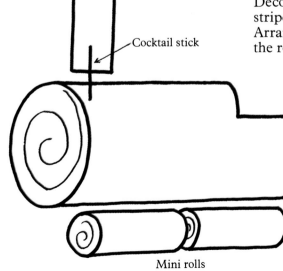

Cocktail stick

Mini rolls

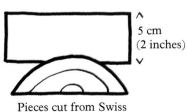

5 cm (2 inches)

Pieces cut from Swiss roll

GATEAUX

Spectacular gâteaux can be served as desserts for buffet and dinner parties as well as providing the centrepiece for a special tea party. Most of them will freeze successfully, which is an advantage since the base is often a very tender sponge cake.

Praline torten

Metric

1 Vanilla Torten Sponge Cake (see page 23)
1½ quantity praline-flavoured Rich Butter Cream (see page 13)
50 g shelled hazelnuts, sliced
100 g sugar
4 × 15 ml spoons water
Whipped cream to serve

Imperial

1 Vanilla Torten Sponge Cake (see page 23)
1½ quantity praline-flavoured Rich Butter Cream (see page 13)
2 oz shelled hazelnuts, sliced
4 oz sugar
4 tablespoons water
Whipped cream to serve

Cut the cake into four layers and sandwich together with two-thirds of the praline butter cream. Spread one-half of the remaining butter cream around the side and coat with the sliced hazelnuts. Put on a serving plate and coat the top with the remaining butter cream.

Brush a baking sheet with oil. Put the sugar and water in a saucepan and stir over a low heat until the sugar has dissolved. Bring to the boil and boil until golden brown, without stirring. Pour the caramel syrup onto the baking sheet and leave to set.

Just before serving, break the caramel into pieces. Place a ring of caramel pieces around the edge of the torten and some in the centre. Serve with whipped cream.

Black Forest cherry cake

Metric

3-egg quantity chocolate-flavoured Whisked Sponge Cake baked in a 20 cm cake tin (see page 22)
1 × 440 g jar Morello cherries
2 × 15 ml spoons cornflour or arrowroot
300 ml whipping cream
4 × 15 ml spoons Kirsch Chocolate Curls (see page 27)

Imperial

3-egg quantity chocolate-flavoured Whisked Sponge Cake baked in an 8 inch cake tin (see page 22)
1 × 15½ oz jar Morello cherries
2 tablespoons cornflour or arrowroot
½ pint whipping cream
4 tablespoons Kirsch Chocolate Curls (see page 27)

Cut the cake into three layers. Place the bottom layer on a serving plate.

Drain the cherries and put the syrup in a saucepan. Stir in the cornflour or arrowroot and bring to the boil, stirring. Simmer for 2 minutes, then remove from the heat. Reserve six cherries for decoration and stir the remainder into the thickened syrup. Leave to cool.

Whip the cream until it just holds its shape. Put half in a nylon piping bag fitted with a large star tube. Pipe a circle of cream around the edge of the bottom layer of the cake. Spread the thickened cherry mixture in the centre.

Sprinkle half the Kirsch on the underside of the centre layer and place on top of the cherry layer. Spread the top of the centre layer with a little cream. Sprinkle the remaining Kirsch on the underside of the top layer and place over the centre layer.

Cover the cake with the remaining cream from the bowl. Arrange the longest chocolate curls in the centre and press the pieces around the side of the cake with a palette knife. Pipe 12 whirls of cream around the top edge and place a reserved cherry on each alternate whirl. Chill until ready to serve.

Note: A can of cherry pie filling may be used instead of the jar of Morello cherries. In this case, omit the cornflour or arrowroot.

Praline torten; Black Forest cherry cake

Pineapple gâteau

Metric

1 Vanilla Torten Sponge Cake (see page 23)
1 × 350 g can pineapple rings, drained
300 ml double cream
2 × 15 ml spoons milk
50 g flaked almonds
4 rounded 15 ml spoons apricot jam
8 glacé cherries
Candied angelica

Imperial

1 Vanilla Torten Sponge Cake (see page 23)
1 × 12 oz can pineapple rings, drained
½ pint double cream
2 tablespoons milk
2 oz flaked almonds
4 rounded tablespoons apricot jam
8 glacé cherries
Candied angelica

Cut the torten into three layers. Cut three pineapple rings in halves and chop the remainder. Put the cream and milk in a bowl and whisk until the cream just holds its shape. Put 3 large spoonsful of cream into a nylon piping bag fitted with a small star tube.

Put the almonds in a grill pan and toast under a moderate grill until evenly browned.

Put the bottom layer of torten on a plate and spread with half of the apricot jam and chopped pineapple and one-third of the cream. Put the second cake layer on top and repeat. Replace the top layer of the torten and spread the top and sides evenly with the remaining cream.

Coat the side of the gâteau with the toasted flaked almonds. Arrange the pineapple halves on top of the gâteau radiating from the centre to the edge. Place a cherry in the centre of each slice.

Pipe a swirl of cream in the centre and one in between each slice of pineapple. Pipe three stars on the edge in between each swirl. Cut two glacé cherries each into six pieces and place a piece on each centre star around the edge and the remainder in the centre.

Cut nine diamond shapes of angelica and place on the swirls of cream. Chill until ready to serve.

Note: This gâteau may be frozen after decorating. Open freeze until firm, then pack in a rigid box. Store for up to 2 months. Thaw in the refrigerator.

Tipsy orange ring

Metric

100 g quantity orange-flavoured Quick Mix Cake mixture, baked in a 20 cm ring mould (see pages 20–21)

Syrup:
100 g granulated sugar
125 ml water
Juice of 1 medium orange
2 × 15 ml spoons orange-flavoured liqueur or medium sherry

Decoration:
2 medium oranges
100 g black grapes, halved and seeded
2 × 15 ml spoons apricot jam, boiled and sieved

Imperial

4 oz quantity orange-flavoured Quick Mix Cake mixture, baked in an 8 inch ring mould (see pages 20–21)

Syrup:
4 oz granulated sugar
¼ pint water
Juice of 1 medium orange
2 tablespoons orange-flavoured liqueur or medium sherry

Decoration:
2 medium oranges
4 oz black grapes, halved and seeded
2 tablespoons apricot jam, boiled and sieved

Put the sugar and water for the syrup in a saucepan and stir over a low heat until the sugar has dissolved. Bring to the boil and boil rapidly for 1 minute without stirring. Remove from the heat and cool. Add the orange juice and liqueur or sherry to the syrup.

Replace the cake in the ring mould in which it was baked and pour over the syrup. Leave in the mould until all the syrup has been absorbed, then invert the cake onto a serving plate.

Scrub one of the oranges and cut half into thin slices. Loosen the segments of the remaining half with a knife, then remove. Cut the peel and pith from the remaining orange with a sharp or serrated knife. Cut in between the membrane to remove the orange segments.

To decorate, fold two orange slices in half, then in half again. Cut the remaining orange slices in halves and arrange them around the cake with a halved grape in each. Place an orange segment in between each. Arrange orange segments and halved grapes alternately around the centre hole of the cake ring and pile the remaining fruit in the centre. Place the folded orange slices on the top. Brush the cake and fruit with apricot jam to glaze.

Pineapple gâteau; Tipsy orange ring

Raspberry meringue carousel

Metric	Imperial
3 egg whites	3 egg whites
200 g icing sugar	7 oz icing sugar
Pink food colouring	Pink food colouring
1 metre 1-cm wide pink ribbon	1 yard ½-inch wide pink ribbon

Filling:	Filling:
250 ml double cream	8 fl oz double cream
250 ml single cream	8 fl oz single cream
350 g raspberries	12 oz raspberries

Cooking time: 2–3 hours
Oven: 110°C, 225°F, Gas Mark ¼

Place a sheet of non-stick baking parchment on two baking sheets. Draw two 18 cm (7 inch) circles on one sheet and invert the paper.

Whisk the egg whites and icing sugar together in a heatproof bowl over a saucepan of hot but not boiling water until the mixture is thick and the whisk leaves a trail when lifted. Remove from the pan and whisk until cool. Spread half of the mixture to fill the two circles on the paper. Put half of the remaining mixture into a nylon piping bag fitted with a medium star tube. Pipe 3.5 cm (1½ inch) lines of meringue on the second baking sheet.

Colour the remaining meringue pale pink with food colouring and pipe lines of pink meringue on the baking sheet. Dry out in a preheated very cool oven for 2 to 3 hours or until the meringues will lift easily off the paper.

Whisk the creams together until they just hold their shape. Put 2 large spoonsful in a nylon piping bag fitted with a medium star tube. Put two-thirds of the remaining cream into a bowl and stir in 250 g (8 oz) of the raspberries.

Sandwich the two meringue layers with the raspberry mixture. Spread the side of the gâteau with the plain cream and place alternate pink and white meringue fingers around the side. Tie the ribbon around.

Pipe a row of stars around the top edge. Arrange a circle of raspberries inside the stars. Repeat with another circle of cream and raspberries. Pipe a swirl of cream in the centre.

Caramel apricot gâteau

Metric	Imperial
Choux Pastry:	Choux Pastry:
50 g margarine	2 oz margarine
125 ml water	¼ pint water
75 g plain flour, sifted	2½ oz plain flour, sifted
2 eggs, beaten	2 eggs, beaten

Base:	Base:
150 g plain flour	6 oz plain flour
50 g caster sugar	2 oz caster sugar
100 g margarine or butter	4 oz margarine or butter

Caramel:	Caramel:
175 g granulated sugar	6 oz granulated sugar
150 ml water	¼ pint water

Filling:	Filling:
250 ml double cream	8 fl oz double cream
250 ml single cream	8 fl oz single cream
1 × 15 ml spoon caster sugar	1 tablespoon caster sugar
1 × 425 g can apricot halves, drained	1 × 15 oz can apricot halves, drained

Cooking time: About 1¼ hours
Oven: 200°C, 400°F, Gas Mark 6
      160°C, 325°F, Gas Mark 3

To make the choux pastry, put the margarine and water in a saucepan. Bring to the boil, then remove from the heat and add the flour all at once. Beat well with a wooden spoon until the mixture forms a ball. Beat in the eggs a little at a time.

Put the mixture into a nylon piping bag fitted with a 1 cm (⅝ inch) plain tube. Pipe small balls of mixture onto a greased baking sheet. Bake in the centre of a preheated moderately hot oven for 30 to 35 minutes or until browned. Transfer the balls to a wire rack and slit each to allow the steam to escape. Cool. Reduce the oven temperature to moderate.

To make the base, place the flour and sugar into a bowl and rub in the fat. Knead to form a soft dough, then roll out and trim to a 20 × 10 cm (8 × 4 inch) oblong. Place on a greased baking sheet and bake in the moderate oven for 35 to 40 minutes or until lightly browned. Transfer to a plate and allow to cool.

To make the caramel, put the sugar and water in a saucepan and stir over a low heat to dissolve the sugar. Bring to the boil and boil rapidly, without stirring, for 6 to 8 minutes or until the syrup turns a rich golden brown. Remove from the heat. Dip the tops of the choux balls into the caramel to coat.

Whisk the creams and caster sugar together until thick. Spread the base with some of the cream and top with the apricot halves. Put the remaining cream in a nylon piping bag fitted with a small star tube. Pipe cream into each choux ball and arrange in two rows around the base of the gâteau.

Pipe a row of stars on top of the apricots next to the choux balls. Serve the extra choux balls separately.

Raspberry meringue carousel; Caramel apricot gâteau

Chocolate rose leaf gâteau

Metric

1 Vanilla Torten Sponge Cake (see page 23)

Chocolate icing:
175 g plain chocolate
100 ml milk

Filling and Decoration:
250 ml double cream
1 × 15 ml spoon milk
4 × 15 ml spoons apricot jam
8 large Chocolate Rose Leaves (see page 27)
16 small Chocolate Rose Leaves (see page 27)

Imperial

1 Vanilla Torten Sponge Cake (see page 23)

Chocolate icing:
6 oz plain chocolate
3 fl oz milk

Filling and Decoration:
8 fl oz double cream
1 tablespoon milk
4 tablespoons apricot jam
8 large Chocolate Rose Leaves (see page 27)
16 small Chocolate Rose Leaves (see page 27)

Cut the cake into three layers.

Break up the chocolate and put in a saucepan with the milk. Heat very gently until the chocolate has melted, stirring occasionally. Remove from the heat and allow to cool.

Put the cream and milk into a bowl and whisk until the cream just holds its shape. Put 2 rounded 15 ml spoons (2 rounded tablespoons) of the cream in a nylon piping bag fitted with a medium star tube.

Spread the bottom layer of the cake with half of the jam and cream. Put the centre layer of the cake on top and spread with the remaining jam and cream. Replace the top layer and place the cake on a wire rack over a plate.

When the chocolate icing is thick enough to coat the back of a spoon, pour it over the cake. Use a small palette knife to spread the side with icing. Leave until the icing has set, then place the gâteau on a serving plate.

Pipe eight scrolls of cream from the centre to the edge on top of the gâteau. Pipe two stars of cream in between each scroll around the top edge. Pipe stars of cream around the base, below the stars on the top.

Arrange eight large chocolate rose leaves on the top of the gâteau in each scroll and the remaining 16 small leaves, in pairs, around the base of the gâteau in the cream stars. Chill until ready to serve.

Mocha japonnaise gâteau

Metric

50 g quantity coffee-flavoured Quick Mix Cake mixture, baked in an 18 cm sandwich tin (see pages 20–21)

Japonnaise:
100 g plain Madeira cake, crumbled
50 g cornflour
125 g caster sugar
3 egg whites
1 × 5 ml spoon instant coffee powder
1 × 5 ml spoon boiling water

Syrup:
100 g granulated sugar
1 × 15 ml spoon cocoa powder
125 ml water

Decoration:
125 g plain chocolate, melted
250 ml double cream
1 × 15 ml spoon milk

Imperial

2 oz quantity coffee-flavoured Quick Mix Cake mixture, baked in a 7 inch sandwich tin (see pages 20–21)

Japonnaise:
4 oz plain Madeira cake, crumbled
2 oz cornflour
5 oz caster sugar
3 egg whites
1 teaspoon instant coffee powder
1 teaspoon boiling water

Syrup:
4 oz granulated sugar
1 tablespoon cocoa powder
¼ pint water

Decoration:
4 oz plain chocolate, melted
8 fl oz double cream
1 tablespoon milk

Cooking time: About 35 minutes
Oven: 160°C, 325°F, Gas Mark 3

Line two baking sheets with non-stick baking parchment. Draw an 18 cm (7 inch) circle on each piece of parchment. Mix the Madeira cake with the cornflour and 75 g (3 oz) of the caster sugar. Whisk the egg whites until stiff. Add the remaining caster sugar and the coffee dissolved in the boiling water. Whisk until stiff; fold in the crumb mixture. Put one-third of the Japonnaise in a nylon piping bag fitted with a 2 cm (⅜ inch) plain tube. Pipe 20 lines, each 5 cm (2 inches) long, around the circles on the parchment. Spread the remaining Japonnaise mixture in the circles to fill. Bake in a preheated moderate oven for 20 to 25 minutes for the fingers and 30 to 35 minutes for the circles. Remove from the parchment and cool on a wire rack.

Put the ingredients for the syrup in a saucepan and bring to the boil, stirring to dissolve the sugar. Boil for 1 minute, then remove from the heat. Replace the Quick mix cake in the tin in which it was baked and soak with the syrup.

Spread the base of both Japonnaise circles with melted chocolate and put the remaining chocolate in a greaseproof paper piping bag. Snip the point from the end and pipe zig-zag threads onto each Japonnaise finger and the top of one of the circles.

Whisk the cream and milk together until the cream just holds its shape. Place a large spoonful of cream in a nylon piping bag fitted with a small star tube. Place one Japonnaise circle, chocolate-coated side up, on a serving plate and spread with one-third of the cream. Invert the soaked Quick mix cake on top and spread with another third of the cream. Cover with the remaining Japonnaise circle with the zig-zag design uppermost. Spread the remaining cream on the side of the gâteau and press the piped Japonnaise fingers into the cream. Pipe swirls of cream around the top edge of the gâteau.

Chocolate rose leaf gâteau; Mocha japonnaise gâteau

Coffee walnut gâteau

Metric

3-egg quantity Whisked
Sponge Cake, flavoured
with 25 g chopped
walnuts and baked in a
20 cm round cake tin
(see page 22)
½ quantity coffee-
flavoured Butter Icing
(see page 13)
Coffee-flavoured Glacé
Icing, made with 225 g
icing sugar (see page 13)
6 walnut halves
Whipped cream to serve

Imperial

3-egg quantity Whisked
Sponge Cake, flavoured
with 1 oz chopped
walnuts and baked in an
8 inch round cake tin
(see page 22)
½ quantity coffee-
flavoured Butter Icing
(see page 13)
Coffee-flavoured Glacé
Icing, made with 8 oz
icing sugar (see page 13)
6 walnut halves
Whipped cream to serve

Make the cake a day before it is required, if possible, to make it easy to split.

Cut the cake into three layers, then sandwich together with Butter icing. Place the cake on a rack with a plate underneath.

Pour the glacé icing over, spreading quickly with a palette knife. Leave for several hours for the icing to set, then carefully loosen the icing at the base and place the gâteau on a serving plate. Lightly press the walnuts around the edge of the gâteau. Serve with whipped cream.

Note: Alternatively, replace the glacé icing with coffee-flavoured Fudge Frosting (see page 15).

Devil's food cake

Metric

100 g quantity chocolate-
flavoured Quick Mix
Cake mixture baked in
2 × 18 cm sandwich tins
(see pages 20–21)
½ quantity vanilla-
flavoured Butter Icing
(see page 13)
1 quantity Quick
American Frosting
(see page 15)
Chocolate Triangles
(see page 27)

Syrup:
2 × 15 ml spoons black
treacle
1 × 5 ml spoon ground
cinnamon
1 × 15 ml spoon cocoa
powder
2 × 15 ml spoons dark
rum or sherry

Imperial

4 oz quantity chocolate-
flavoured Quick Mix
Cake mixture baked in
2 × 7 inch sandwich tins
(see pages 20–21)
½ quantity vanilla-
flavoured Butter Icing
(see page 13)
1 quantity Quick
American Frosting
(see page 15)
Chocolate Triangles
(see page 27)

Syrup:
2 tablespoons black
treacle
1 teaspoon ground
cinnamon
1 tablespoon cocoa
powder
2 tablespoons dark
rum or sherry

Heat the syrup ingredients together in a saucepan until well mixed, then remove from the heat. Sprinkle the syrup over the base of each cake and leave to soak for about 1 hour. Sandwich the cakes with Butter icing and place on a serving plate.

Cover the side and then the top with frosting. Swirl the frosting and pull up into peaks. Leave to set, then arrange chocolate triangles upright in the centre. Frost the cake the day it is required.

Coffee walnut gâteau; Devil's food cake

Lemon cheesecake gâteau

Metric

3-egg quantity Whisked Sponge Cake, baked in 2 × 20 cm sandwich tins (see page 22)

Filling:
250 g full fat soft cheese
1 large can sweetened condensed milk
120 ml lemon juice

Decoration:
120 ml double cream
1 × 15 ml spoon milk
1 small lemon

Imperial

3-egg quantity Whisked Sponge Cake, baked in 2 × 8 inch sandwich tins (see page 22)

Filling:
8 oz full fat soft cheese
1 large can sweetened condensed milk
4 fl oz lemon juice

Decoration:
4 fl oz double cream
1 tablespoon milk
1 small lemon

To make the filling, beat the soft cheese until smooth. Gradually beat in the sweetened condensed milk followed by the lemon juice and beat until thickened. (Bottled lemon juice can be used, but if using the juice from fresh lemons, add 2 × 5 ml spoons (2 teaspoons) finely grated lemon rind.) Spread half the filling over the top of each cake layer and leave for 10 minutes to set.

Whip the cream and milk together until it stands in soft peaks. Put in a nylon piping bag fitted with a large star tube. Cut six slices from the centre of the lemon. Cut four into halves and two into quarters.

Place one cake layer on a serving plate. Mark the top of the other layer into eight sections. With a long 'tail' on each marked line, pipe a swirl of cream from the edge towards the centre.

To decorate, arrange a quarter slice of lemon at an angle on each 'tail' of cream. Cut each halved lemon slice from the centre to the rind and twist each side in an opposite direction. Place between each swirl of cream at the edge. Use a palette knife or a slice to lift carefully onto the bottom layer of the gâteau. Chill until ready to serve.

Note: This cheesecake freezes well. Omit the fresh lemon decoration and open freeze for 2 hours. Wrap in foil and store for up to 3 months. To use, unwrap, place on a serving plate and thaw slowly in the refrigerator. Decorate with fresh lemon slices just before serving.

Peach Melba gâteau

Metric

2-egg quantity Whisked Sponge Cake, baked in an 18 cm square tin (see page 22)

Decoration:
225 g raspberries
3 × 15 ml spoons caster sugar
250 ml double cream
2 × 15 ml spoons milk
50 g flaked almonds, toasted
1 fresh peach, peeled, stoned and sliced, or 8 canned peach slices
2 × 15 ml spoons sugar (optional)
1 × 15 ml spoon lemon juice (optional)

Imperial

2-egg quantity Whisked Sponge Cake, baked in a 7 inch square tin (see page 22)

Decoration:
8 oz raspberries
3 tablespoons caster sugar
8 fl oz double cream
2 tablespoons milk
2 oz flaked almonds, toasted
1 fresh peach, peeled, stoned and sliced, or 8 canned peach slices
2 tablespoons sugar (optional)
1 tablespoon lemon juice (optional)

Trim the cake edges and cut it in half to make two bars. Reserve half of the raspberries for decoration. Press the remainder through a sieve to make a purée. Add the caster sugar and stir until dissolved. Spread three-quarters of the raspberry purée on one cake bar.

Whisk the cream and milk together until it just holds its shape. Put one-third in a piping bag fitted with a medium star tube. Spread one-third of the remainder over each bar of cake, then sandwich the two together with the raspberry purée and cream layer in the centre.

Spread the sides of the sandwiched bar with the remaining cream, then place it on a sheet of greaseproof paper. Sprinkle the almonds around the sides on the paper, then press them onto the cream, using the paper to lift them. Pipe a row of cream stars along each long side of the top edge of the gâteau and chill until ready to serve.

If using a fresh peach, dissolve the sugar in the lemon juice and a little water in a saucepan. Add the peach slices and cook for 3 minutes. Drain on absorbent kitchen paper and chill.

Arrange the peach slices, rounded sides downwards, in a row along the centre of the bar. With a teaspoon, drizzle a little of the remaining raspberry purée over each slice. Arrange the reserved raspberries at each end of the bar.

Lemon cheesecake gâteau; Peach Melba gâteau

SMALL CAKES

When catering for a crowd, small cakes are the easiest to serve. Some of these can be made in quantity for the local fête, but there are also cakes suitable for the smartest afternoon tea.

Iced gems

Metric	Imperial
3-egg quantity Whisked Sponge Cake, baked in a 28 × 18 × 3.5 cm tin (see page 22)	*3-egg quantity Whisked Sponge Cake, baked in an 11 × 7 × 1½ inch tin (see page 22)*
Apricot jam, boiled and sieved	*Apricot jam, boiled and sieved*
¼ quantity Almond Paste (see page 32)	*¼ quantity Almond Paste (see page 32)*
750 g icing sugar	*1½ lb icing sugar*
Food colourings	*Food colourings*
Decoration:	*Decoration:*
Mimosa balls	*Mimosa balls*
Chocolate beans	*Chocolate beans*
Orange and lemon jelly slices	*Orange and lemon jelly slices*

Use a day-old cake, if possible. Invert the cake onto a board. Trim the edges and brush the cake with jam. Roll out the Almond paste to fit the cake. Invert the cake onto the Almond paste and cut around. Reserve the trimmings. Place the cake on a board with the Almond paste uppermost. Cut six 5 cm (2 inch) circles in two rows of three from one end of the cake. Mark the remaining piece of cake along the length into three bars, one 5 cm (2 inches) wide, the centre one 6 cm (2½ inches) wide and the other 4 cm (1½ inches) wide. Cut three 5 cm (2 inch) squares from the first bar, then cut diagonally across to make six triangles. Cut the centre bar into six 2.5 cm (1 inch) oblongs, and the last bar into four 4 cm (1½ inch) squares. Knead the Almond paste trimmings together and make different shaped pieces. Put these on some of the cakes.

Make glacé icing by mixing 500 g (1 lb) of the icing sugar with enough boiling water so that the icing thickly coats the back of the spoon. Put the bowl of icing in a saucepan of boiling water off the heat.

Assemble food colourings, a skewer and another bowl in a saucepan of boiling water.

Place one of each shape of cake on a wire rack over a plate. Coat with the glacé icing, using a large spoon to pour the icing over. When the icing has stopped falling, carefully transfer the cakes to a board. Leave to set.

Put half the remaining icing in the second heated bowl. Tint the icing pink by adding drops of colouring with the skewer. Coat four more cakes with pink icing. Add a little blue or purple colouring to the pink icing to make it mauve. Mix gently, then coat four more cakes.

Tint the remaining white icing pale yellow and coat four more cakes. Divide the yellow icing into two. Tint one-half orange, adding red colouring, and one-half green, adding green or blue colouring. Coat three cakes with orange icing and three with green.

Add more colouring then icing sugar to the mauve icing to make a piping consistency. Pipe stars and shells on the white cakes with a No. 43 tube in a paper piping bag. Mix remaining icing sugar with boiling water to a piping consistency. Fill a greaseproof paper piping bag with icing and snip off the point. Pipe threads of icing across some of the cakes. Pipe stars or shells using a number 6 star tube in a piping bag on the remaining cakes. Decorate with mimosa balls, chocolate beans and candied orange and lemon slices. *Makes 22 small cakes*

Cutting diagram for iced gems

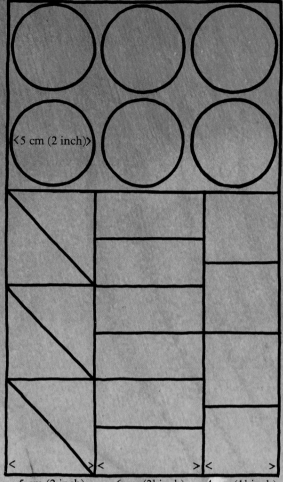

‹5 cm (2 inch)›

5 cm (2 inch) 6 cm (2½ inch) 4 cm (1½ inch)

Bitter orange chocolate boxes

Metric	Imperial
50 g quantity orange-flavoured Quick Mix Cake mixture, baked in an 18 cm square tin (see pages 20–21) for 20 to 25 minutes	2 oz quantity orange-flavoured Quick Mix Cake mixture, baked in a 7 inch square tin (see pages 20–21) for 20 to 25 minutes
Thick-cut marmalade	Thick-cut marmalade
175 g plain chocolate-flavoured cake covering	6 oz plain chocolate-flavoured cake covering
1 quantity orange-flavoured Butter Icing (see page 13)	1 quantity orange-flavoured Butter Icing (see page 13)

Cut the cake into two layers and sandwich together with marmalade. Trim the sides and ends and cut the cake into eighteen 3 cm (1¼ inch) squares.

Draw two 23 cm (9 inch) squares on non-stick vegetable parchment. Mark 3.5 cm (1½ inch) sections on the outside of each square.

Melt the chocolate cake covering and spread in the marked sections. Leave to set, then cut into thirty-six 3.5 cm (1½ inch) chocolate squares as directed on page 27.

To assemble the cakes, secure four chocolate squares around each square of cake with a little Butter icing (hold the chocolate squares by the edges to avoid making the chocolate dull).

Pipe a swirl of Butter icing on the top of each cake and decorate with a piece of chunky peel from the marmalade. Chill until ready to serve.

Makes 18 cakes

Chocolate ginger cups

Metric	Imperial
100 g chocolate-flavoured cake covering	4 oz chocolate-flavoured cake covering
Filling:	Filling:
4 pieces stem ginger	4 pieces stem ginger
4 trifle sponge cakes, crumbled	4 trifle sponge cakes, crumbled
2 × 15 ml spoons ginger syrup	2 tablespoons ginger syrup
150 ml whipping cream	¼ pint whipping cream

Melt the chocolate in a heatproof bowl over a saucepan of hot water. Place 2 × 5 ml spoons (2 teaspoons) of the melted chocolate in each of 8 greaseproof cake cases and spread quickly to coat the base and side evenly. Leave the chocolate to set and harden in the refrigerator, then peel off the greaseproof paper.

Cut eight slices of ginger for decoration, then chop the remainder. Mix the chopped ginger with the sponge cake and ginger syrup (from the jar). Divide between the chocolate cases.

Whip the cream until just thick. Put in a nylon piping bag fitted with a large star tube and pipe a swirl of cream into each case. Decorate each with the reserved ginger.

Makes 8 chocolate cups

Iced lemon and cherry bars

Metric

*100 g quantity Quick
Mix Cake mixture, baked
in a 28 × 18 cm oblong
tin (see pages 20–21) for
20 to 25 minutes
Lemon curd
Raspberry jam
1 quantity Butter Icing
(see page 13)
Grated rind and juice of
½ lemon
Vanilla essence
Yellow and pink food
colourings*

*Decoration:
50 g desiccated coconut
2 orange and lemon jelly
slices, each cut into 4
pieces
4 glacé cherries, halved*

Imperial

*4 oz quantity Quick
Mix Cake mixture, baked
in an 11 × 7 inch oblong
tin (see pages 20–21) for
20 to 25 minutes
Lemon curd
Raspberry jam
1 quantity Butter Icing
(see page 13)
Grated rind and juice of
½ lemon
Vanilla essence
Yellow and pink food
colourings*

*Decoration:
2 oz desiccated coconut
2 orange and lemon jelly
slices, each cut into 4
pieces
4 glacé cherries, halved*

Trim the edges of the cake, then cut the cake in half down the length. Cut each piece into two layers. Sandwich one piece with lemon curd and the other with raspberry jam. Divide the Butter icing into two. Flavour one half with the lemon rind and juice and the other with a few drops of vanilla essence. Add a little yellow colouring to the lemon-flavoured icing and pink colouring to 4 × 15 ml spoons (4 tablespoons) of the vanilla icing.

Spread the top and sides of the lemon curd cake with some of the lemon icing and the other piece with the uncoloured vanilla icing. Dip the sides of the lemon cake into half the coconut to coat. Toast the remaining coconut under the grill. Cool, then use to coat the vanilla cake.

Put the remaining lemon icing into a piping bag fitted with a No. 7 star tube. Pipe whirls of icing along each long side of the lemon-iced cake. Cut into eight bars and decorate each with a piece of orange or lemon jelly slice.

Using a palette knife, put the remaining uncoloured vanilla icing in one half of a piping bag fitted with a No. 7 star tube. Put the pink icing down the other side. Pipe coils of icing down each long side of the vanilla-iced cake. Cut into eight bars and decorate each with a halved glacé cherry.
Makes 16 cakes

Petal cakes

Metric	Imperial
50 g quantity vanilla-flavoured Quick Mix Cake mixture, baked in 9 paper cake cases (see pages 20–21)	2 oz quantity vanilla-flavoured Quick Mix Cake mixture, baked in 9 paper cake cases (see pages 20–21)
Clear honey	Clear honey
100 g Almond Paste (see page 32)	4 oz Almond Paste (see page 32)
Food colouring (optional)	Food colouring (optional)
Coloured silver balls	Coloured silver balls

Brush the top of each cake with honey. Colour the Almond paste, if desired, then roll out on a board sprinkled with cornflour. Cut into 36 small circles. Pinch each at one side to form a petal shape, then place four on each cake in a flower design. Brush each 'petal' with honey and place some coloured silver balls in the centre of each.

Makes 9 cakes

Mushroom cakes

Metric	Imperial
175 g Almond Paste (see page 32)	6 oz Almond Paste (see page 32)
Apricot jam, boiled and sieved	Apricot jam, boiled and sieved
50 g quantity chocolate-flavoured Quick Mix Cake mixture, baked in 9 tartlet tins (see pages 20–21)	2 oz quantity chocolate-flavoured Quick Mix Cake mixture, baked in 9 tartlet tins (see pages 20–21)
Chocolate-flavoured Butter Icing, made with 50 g icing sugar, 25 g butter and 1 × 2.5 ml spoon lemon juice (see page 13)	Chocolate-flavoured Butter Icing, made with 2 oz icing sugar, 1 oz butter and ½ teaspoon lemon juice (see page 13)

Roll out the Almond paste thinly and cut into 8.5 cm (3½ inch) circles. Gather up the trimmings and re-roll, if necessary, to make nine circles, but reserve some Almond paste to make 'stalks'.

Brush each circle of paste with apricot jam. Place a cake in the centre of each and mould the Almond paste around each cake.

Spread the top of each cake with icing. Mark with a fork, then place a stalk in the centre of each.

Makes 9 cakes

Butterfly cakes

Metric

100 g quantity chocolate-
flavoured Quick Mix
Cake mixture, baked in
18 paper cases
(see pages 20–21)
Butter Icing, made with
150 g icing sugar, 75 g
butter and 1.5 × 5 ml
spoons lemon juice
(see page 13)
Icing sugar

Imperial

4 oz quantity chocolate-
flavoured Quick Mix
Cake mixture, baked in
18 paper cases
(see pages 20–21)
Butter Icing, made with
6 oz icing sugar, 3 oz
butter and 1½ teaspoons
lemon juice
(see page 13)
Icing sugar

Cut the top off each cake, cutting into the cake at an angle.
Cut the tops in half and reserve.
Put a little Butter icing in the centre of each cake. Fit a
piping bag with a small star tube and fill with the remaining
icing. Pipe three shells on two sides of the cut-out part of
each cake. Press the reserved cut pieces of cake into the
icing in the centre above each row of shells to form 'wings'.
Put a little icing sugar in a sieve and gently shake a little
over each cake.
Makes 18 cakes

Top hats

Metric

100 g quantity vanilla-
flavoured Quick Mix
Cake mixture, baked in
18 paper cake cases
(see pages 20–21)
2 × 15 ml spoons red
jam, sieved
1 quantity Butter Icing
(see page 13)

Imperial

4 oz quantity vanilla-
flavoured Quick Mix
Cake mixture, baked in
18 paper cake cases
(see pages 20–21)
2 tablespoons red jam,
sieved
1 quantity Butter Icing
(see page 13)

Cut a small circle, about 2 cm (¾ inch) in diameter, from the
centre of each cake. Spread the top of each cake circle with
jam.
Place a little jam in each hole. Fit a piping bag with a small
star tube and fill with Butter icing. Pipe a double wall of
icing around each hole, then lightly press a 'hat' on top.
Makes 18 cakes

95

Index

PDO 81-490